WALKO

THE TAINTED TOUR OF 1956

Gareth Cartman

Contents

Introduction	v
The Teams	vii
A Man In A Hurry	1
Belgium Attacks, Bidot Worries	9
Nine Men Stay Away For The Day	15
An Alsatian Among The Bretons	19
Brittany First	31
The Yellow Jersey, The Level Crossing, & the Invisible Man	37
The Water Carrier, the Saviour, and the Protector	43
Why do they have to go so fast?	51
Hassen-le-Magnifique	59
Enter (and exit) Pierrette Walkowiak	67
Operation "Lose the Yellow Jersey"	71
So, Charly Gaul, Do You Have It?	77
Jempy Schmitz's Awesome Adventure	83
Treason Among the Tricolores	89
Little Louis and the Breakawee	97
The Physician, The Belgians, and the Fishy Excuses	105
None The Wiser, Nothing By Half	111
Dotto and Lerda leave Laurédi in the lurch	117
The Revival of Charly Gaul, and the Man Who Wasn't There	123
The Attack They All Missed	133
The Crash, the Bandit, the Pursuit	139
Déjeuner sur l'herbe, or Walko's Time Trials	147
Leave Me Here in Montluçon, My Dear	153
Take Me Back to Montluçon	163
Final Thoughts - Epilogue	171

Introduction
The 1956 Tour de France

We have been spoiled, since the war. An age of gladiators on wheels has given us the greats such as Fausto Coppi, Gino Bartali, Ferdy Kübler and Hugo Koblet. For the last three years, the Tour has been dominated by Louison Bobet, and were it not for saddle sores that he feared had become cancerous, Bobet would have been riding - and winning - his fourth Tour de France. Alas, Bobet was reduced to making his debut as a journalist, leaving a French team leaderless and rudderless.

You could argue that Bobet's absence is what makes the 1956 Tour de France so fascinating. With the French team unable to decide who is their nominated successor to Bobet, and with the Italians unable to decide who should succeed the ageing Coppi, almost every rider on the start line at Reims could imagine himself wearing the yellow jersey.

This is only a slight exaggeration. The media was unsure of how to pitch this coming Tour. Would a new hero reveal himself? Would someone like Nello Laurédi win now that his chief antagonist Bobet is out of the way? To suggest that Laurédi, riding for one of the regional teams, might win the Tour, is almost heresy. And yet in their struggle to predict this most unpredictable of Tours, journalists are hedging their bets.

What many didn't appreciate at the time was how pivotal the 1956 Tour would be. For years, the majority of the peloton had paled in comparison to the gang of four - Coppi, Bobet and the two Swiss K's. But cycling was getting quicker. More athletic. And what's more, rule changes signalled a move away from the Desgranges-era regulations which forced riders to repair their own punctures. A flat tyre could be replaced from the team car, or from a teammate. Symbolised by this one simple rule change, cycling was being transformed. An era of heroes gritting it out in epic battles was quietly being ushered out, and a more athletic, technical era was about to begin. No more repairing your bike in a forge, no more goggles and inner tubes over the shoulders - the fastest man wins.

And yet, despite rule changes and the coming of a supposed new era, the Tour de France somehow remains the same. 5,000km around France, dipping in and out of Belgium and Italy whenever it takes its fancy, the Tour is part of the France's soul. Alternating between clockwise and anti-clockwise, each Tour takes in the Alps and the Pyrenees, and more often than not, the Massif Centrale in between. Small towns and villages along the route spend days preparing for a fleeting glimpse of their heroes, and a further day cleaning up the mess. Every year, the Tour is the same, and yet it is changing constantly.

Walko is a collection of short stories as much as it is the tale of a Tour that its organisers claimed to be one of their favourite Tours of all time. Unpredictable, controversial, with no shortage of heroics and skullduggery. A Tour like any other, but not so. And at the heart of it, one man who could seriously lay claim to being the only man who didn't believe he could win at the start line in Reims.

The Teams

France

Blue, White & Red shirts

Pierre BARBOTIN, Gilbert BAUVIN, Louis BERGAUD, André DARRIGADE, Jean FORESTIER, Raphaël GEMINIANI, François MAHE, Jean MALLEJAC, René PRIVAT, Antonin ROLLAND

Technical Director: Marcel BIDOT

Italy

Red, White & Green shirts

Pierino BAFFI, Agostino COLETTO, Angelo CONTERNO, Nino DEFILIPPIS, Allesandro FANTINI, Pasquale FORNARA, Pietro GIUDICI, Bruno MONTI, Gastone NENCINI, Arrigo PADOVAN

Technical Director: Alfredo BINDA

Belgium

Light Blue shirts with Black, Yellow & Red Band

Jean ADRIAENSSENS, Jean BRANKART, Alex CLOSE, Alfred DE BRUYNE, Gilbert DESMET, Raymond IM-PANIS, Marcel JANSSENS, Stan OCKERS, Richard VAN GENECHTEN, André VLAEYEN

Technical Director: Sylvère MAES

Holland

Orange shirts with Red, White & Blue Band

Daan DE GROOT, Joseph HINSON, Jef LAHAYE, Jean NOLTEN, Wies STOLKER, Piet VAN DE BREKEL, Arie VAN DER PLUYM, Wiel VAN DONGEN, Gerrit VOORTING, Wout WAGTMANS

Technical Director: Kees PELLENAERS

Spain

Grey shirt, Red, Yellow and Red Band

Federico BAHAMONTES, Salvador BOTELLA, Miguel BOVER, Miguel CHACON, Jesus LORENO, René MARIGIL, Carmelo MORALES, Miguel POBLET, Bernado RUIZ, José SERRA

Technical Director: Luis Puig ESTEVE

Switzerland

Red Shirt, White cross

Werner ARNOLD, Jack BOVAY, Claude FREI, Jean-Claude GRET, Hans HOLLENSTEIN, Fausto LURATTI, Rémo PIANEZZI, Fritz SCHAER, Max SCHELLEMBERG, Ernst TRAXEL

Technical Director: Alex BURTIN

LUXEMBOURG (MIXED)

Red Shirts with White & Light Blue Band

Antonio BARBOSA, Aldo BOLZAN, Marcel ERNZER, Charly GAUL, Edmond JACOBS, Willy KEMP, Nicolas MORN, Brian ROBINSON, Jean SCHMIT, Jean-Pierre SCHMITZ

Technical Director: Nicolas FRANTZ

North-East-Centre (Nord-Est-Centre)

Violet shirts, two white bands

Ugo ANZILE, Mano BERTOLO, Roger CHUPIN, Adolphe DELEDDA, Camille HUYGHE, Pierre PARDOEN, Raymond REISSER, Gilbert SCODELLER, Pierre SCRIBANTE, Roger WALKOWIAK

Technical Director: Sauveur Ducazeaux

South-East (Sud-Est)

Royal Blue, two gold bands

Roger CHAUSSABEL, Jean DOTTO, Raymond ELENA, José GIL, Nello LAUREDI, Jean LERDA, Raymond MEYZENQ, Joseph MIRANDO, Vinvent VITETTA

Technical Director: Marius GUIRAMAND

West (Ouest)

White shirts with two blue bands

Armand AUDAIRE, Arthur BIHANNIC, Roger HASSENFORDER, Louis CAPUT, Claude LE BER, Eugène LETENDRE, Joseph MORVAN, Fernand PICOT, Maurice QUENTIN, Joseph THOMIN

Technical Director: Léon LE CALVEZ

Ile-de-France

Red shirts with two white bands

Nicolas BARONE, Stanislas BOBER, Seamus ELLIOTT, René FOURNIER, Raymond HOORELBEKE, Jean LE GUILLY, Francis SIGUENZA, Jean SKERL, Alfred TOMELLO

Technical Director: Jean PRUNIER

A Man In A Hurry
5th July 1956
Stage 1, Reims to Liège, 223km

Under a cloud

André Darrigade has the look of a man brought up under a burning sun. Stocky, square-jawed, sun-tanned and – usually – of bright disposition, Darrigade is France's great sprinting hope. Some would say (André included) that he's more than that. They'd call him a routier-sprinter, fast at the finish but more than capable of organising a peloton and chasing down breakaways.

Andre is from the Landes region of France, a land of duck fat and goose liver, of sunlit uplands and cornfields, of hearty meals and heartier wines. And while all around André have lived life at the languid pace the temperature often demands of them, André has lived his life in a hurry. Nothing could happen quickly enough. Which is, if you think about it, apt for a sprinter.

Today however, as the Tour prepares to get underway, André is under a cloud. The team have noticed it, the journalists have made a point of it. His mind is elsewhere. The grey clouds have gathered just for André.

WALKO

Just days ago, his brother Roger – another (lesser) cyclist – had been marched out of the family home on military service. There were tears that day. They came unannounced, as they often do, in their numbers. They filtered into the kitchen and read out their proclamation that Roger Darrigade would be serving with the French army. It's 1956, not 1812, his mother had cried, tears in her eyes, plates broken on the terracotta floor of their farmhouse kitchen. When they call, you can't refuse, and you can't delay. They'll send him to Algeria. Some boys don't come back.

Roger didn't even look over his shoulder.

Roger wasn't alone. Jacques Anquetil had also received the call-up just weeks ago. Jacques and André had become good friends; they had hoped to ride the Tour together. But Jacques wouldn't get Algeria, surely. Someone would put a word in.

This was no way to start a Tour.

Gilbert Bauvin leans across, breaking André's reverie. "Seen those Belgians?" he conspires. "Getting done for logos on their shorts. Goddet's fuming."

André looks across at Stan Ockers who is wearing more logos than the caravane publicitaire. Ah yes, Ockers. Rainbow jersey. Got to watch him, him and his logos.

André checks his shorts.

Bauvin was one of those riders he couldn't wait to see the back of. Or, to be more precise, one of those riders he wanted to show his back to. He wasn't meant to be in the French team this year – it should have been Louison, or any number of other riders. But Gilbert Bauvin was a regional rider, not a tricolore. Fidgeting, André Darrigade turns away from Bauvin and taps his handlebars. Race, damnit, start the race.

No, André was not a patient man. He turned up at the Velodrome d'Hiver in 1950 wearing a pair of loose shorts and a white shirt. He just wanted to race, wanted to show the world beyond his small town or Narrosse that he could ride, and ride fast. No rules against that, they said, laughing.

Round after round went by, the young André winning each one by several bike lengths. They weren't laughing any more. Until he came up against the world champion Maspès. The Italian, who was unbeaten, looked him up and down and mentally chalked up another win, yet another payment in the bank. André beat him on the line, a whole wheel length in front.

Nothing could come quickly enough.

Le Départ

The Tour starts off with a neutralised départ fictif, a leisurely bike ride through the streets of Reims, at first some wide boulevards, a couple of roundabouts and the buildings start to shrink in size. André Darrigade is at the front, avoiding his teammates and avoiding eye contact with any other rider, fixing his eyes on the handlebars and the solitary wheel in front of him.

Outside Reims, Jacques Goddet waves from atop the Peugeot, and the Tour is underway. At last.

Wout Wagtmans, the miniature Dutchman known as De Clown makes the first break for it, only to be hauled in – request for breakaway refused. Voorting, another Dutchman, makes a burst off the front just two kilometres later, only to be reeled back in by Darrigade who is setting a furious pace. At 55km per hour, it's hard to break free. He settles back in alongside his compatriot.

Yes, I tried too. It didn't work.

An actual breakaway would form when Brian Robinson – the only Englishman in the Tour – found a gap and ploughed straight through it. Nello Laurédi entered his slipstream almost by accident and found himself three or four metres ahead of the peloton. Make your mind up time. Darrigade's mind was made up, and his move was the signal for others to join. Voorting, Walkowiak, Barbosa, Van der Pluym, Vlaeyen, Baffi… and Fritz Schär, the dangerous Swiss rider, the last to bridge the gap. Within three kilometres, the peloton had given up hope and the Tour's first breakaway was set.

It is normal for a breakaway to operate in silence. A tacit acknowledgement from each man that in order to stay away, the breakaway must work together and work hard. This, however, is a Darrigade breakaway. Any break with André Darrigade in it is – by definition – a Darrigade breakaway. The last thing any other rider wants is to do all the work and end up being overtaken by Darrigade on the line. So the routier-sprinter has to do the bulk of the work, which means sitting on the front and forcing a pace that would break lesser men.

That pace started to tell. After 77km, the gap to the peloton had extended to 3'35". Once over the Rocroi climb and through the feeding zone, the chalk boards had the gap up to 5 minutes. At the Belgian border, the peloton was an astonishing 8 minutes behind.

Some men succumbed to bike problems. Walkowiak had been looking good but a puncture saw to his chances and the peloton would soon provide him with a home. Voorting and Lauredi had given too much, too soon, and Vlaeyen soon followed with Baffi not far behind.

That left three men…

That left three men: André himself, Brian Robinson and Fritz Schär. A Frenchman, an Englishman, and a German-speaking Swiss.

A Man In A Hurry

It doesn't take a language degree to understand the language of the roadman. A flicked elbow, a shake of the head, an outstretched hand and an exasperated sigh. Darrigade puffs out his cheeks and sucks it up. It's his breakaway.

He looks behind. Robinson, he looks tough but those aren't sprinter's legs. You'd worry about him if you were in a fight though. Riding for Luxembourg this year – the English experiment failed last year, although he still finished 24th and therefore he's a danger. Rides for Raymond Louviot and the St. Raphaël team, so the boy's got some talent. And Charly Gaul must like him if he's riding for Luxembourg.

And if Charly Gaul likes him, then he must be good.

And Schär. He's wily. You have to be wily if you've spent your entire career trying to nick wins from under the noses of Koblet and Kübler. He's worn the yellow jersey before, Darrigade thinks, and he's a doper. Everyone knows he's a doper. Worse than that, he's what the French would call ratagasse – a wheel-sucker. He never participates, he just sits on your wheel and takes the draft. He even looks like a ratagasse. Small, scrawny and balding, the type of B-class rider who lives in the shadows of greater men hoping to pick off the scraps they occasionally throw. Hugo Koblet, now there was a rider. A gentleman, too. Always carried a comb in his back pocket, always had a kind word, and who was always on his wheel, waiting for him to bonk? Old Fritzi Schär.

Beware Schär.

André looks ahead. A break in the clouds at last and André can pretend, in his mind, that he's riding south towards the sun. The gloom of Reims has lifted. Gone are the grey skies of Champagne, blown on the breeze. Belgium has bathed itself in warm, fuzzy yellow sunlight to welcome the Tour. Dinant, it is – a pretty town, cathedral reflected in the Meuse river as the three companions cross the bridge. Its inhabitants had gathered early, decking the town out in yellow, none of them expecting the leaders to pass through what turned out to be a full 36 minutes ahead of schedule. They were still putting up the hanging baskets.

A full ten minutes later, those who had sneaked into the bar and missed the trio of breakaway hopefuls burning up the fresh tarmac would get the opportunity to see the peloton. Fans ten deep hurled their appreciation – some hurled more than that. De Bruyne, Impanis, Ockers, Brankart – our boys! Our boys – ten minutes back.

It took Belgium to make the Tour come alive. As it often does.

Deeper into Belgium they rode. Occasionally, Darrigade would get a break as Schär or Robinson took pity on him and bore some of the workload, each man maintaining that brutal pace that Darrigade had insisted on from morning onwards. The outskirts of Liège took on a more industrial tone as the tarmac deteriorated and straight roads became roundabouts and corners. It's almost as if Liège were still at war. The air was heavier and dirtier than anything the riders had encountered on the route north.

The chalkboards reassured the three men that one of them would be wearing the yellow jersey, and if they were honest with each other, they all knew who. On entering the velodrome, both Robinson and Schär instinctively drop back behind Darrigade. We'll find your slipstream, they imply, and we'll take you on the line.

This, to André, is like a red rag to a bull.

He hits the bank hard and leaves them two, three bike lengths behind. Four, five and six bike lengths and finally they break and there's still half the velodrome to ride.

Of course, André takes the stage, even slowing down as he reaches the line to throw his arms in the air and celebrate. A smile, at last. Schär and Robinson barely have the energy to fight it out for second place. The result was never really in doubt – and if you think about it, the result probably wasn't in doubt from the minute the riders left Reims. Perhaps hindsight is a wonderful thing, but not once did André Darrigade let the pace drop. A procession at 50km per hour.

And so, as André Darrigade pulls on the yellow jersey for the first time in his career, does he have pretentions to take it any further? Does he think it's his to keep? After all, his team director Marcel Bidot had confidently declared that there is no team leader this year. They'll support the man who leads. Find me a leader, he might as well have said, for I have not a clue.

Could that man be André?

No, he would retort. I'm your sprinter. I'm your routier-sprinter. I'm here to win stages, and I'm here to be useful. I'll distract attention from your star riders, whoever they may be this year, and that's my job. I'll stick to it.

André had caught his breath, had a drink and had even carried out some of his first interviews with the press when the peloton belatedly entered the velodrome, a blur of colour and disappointment. The Belgians were meant to win their stage, but they were taken by surprise, unable to get anyone other than Vlaeyen into the first break and he couldn't keep up. Brankart would keep himself for the mountains, but Ockers – the rainbow jersey – where was he?

The Italians, led by the giant Alfredo Binda, were hugely disappointing. They might point to the lack of a Coppi or a Bartali, but Nencini and De Filippis were meant to do better than this. Their race tactics would certainly come in for scrutiny from the local press.

But the truth is that André Darrigade had raced them all off his back wheel. And there were many reasons why this was one of the fastest stages in Tour history. You could point to the roads, as good as they have been since the first World War. Reparations had taken some time, as Liège could attest, but give a man smooth tarmac and you'll hear the hum of skinny tyres and you'll feel the machine take flight. For the first time ever, a puncture could be solved by simply changing a wheel. No need to carry your inner tubes around your shoulders any more.

The frenzy, however, could only really be attributed to the man who rode off his problems. How better to put your worries to one side than to ride the hell out of your bike and make other men suffer?

Belgium Attacks, Bidot Worries
6th July 1956
Stage 2, Liège to Lille, 213km

It wasn't meant to be like this

The Tour rarely makes much of an incursion into foreign territory. A day outside of the Hexagone and that is quite enough. Today, the Tour makes its way back into France with the rather rudimentary cut-through Belgium via Brussels and the Flemish Ardennes. None of this should be too testing, and one man who is doubtless desperate to see home soil is Marcel Bidot, technical director of the French team and a man without a car.

Bidot has spent the morning at the police station, giving as many details as possible about the stolen team car. Yes, officer, the team radio was in it. Insurance papers, too. Glove box. A yellow hat, on the passenger seat. You'll recognise it, it's a Peugeot with Tour de France written all over it. There won't be many of them.

The morning wasn't supposed to pass like this. Bidot had intended to spend an hour with Darrigade, his yellow jersey. Here's our strategy, he was meant to be saying, plotting out in detail the points at which a Belgian (most likely) would make a break, plotting out how Darrigade and his teammates would control the peloton and control the gaps. A defensive day, not an attacking day.

The car was found just before the départ, minus its race radio. He would have to borrow one from the 4CV, just to stay in touch.

Bidot was right about the Belgians. They would rightly have been disappointed yesterday not to have someone like De Bruyne alongside Darrigade, but then again, Darrigade would never have let De Bruyne go with him.

De Bruyne, De Bruyne

Fred De Bruyne is this year's revelation. He started the season winning Paris-Nice by a huge winning margin and followed up with Milan San Remo, beating the Italian favourite Magni by nearly a full minute. As if that wasn't enough, he then took Liege-Bastogne-Liege, La Doyenne, in the sprint against Van Genechten. It was a formality in the end, his opponent acknowledging he didn't have the legs to beat the new king of the Classics.

In fact, it's De Bruyne who makes the first move as the peloton crosses Wallonie, and Marcel Bidot is relieved to see André Darrigade not attempt to bridge the gap. Instead, he sends the Breton Malléjac to monitor the Belgian classics man. Slow him down a bit.

Bidot trusts Malléjac, which puts him in a team of one after last year's shenanigans on Mont Ventoux. Doped up to his eyeballs, Malléjac collapsed 10km from the finish line, one foot still pedalling, sweat lashing from his ashen forehead. In the ambulance, having been given oxygen and having had his jaws forcibly prised apart to take water, it took him 15 minutes to regain consciousness and when he did, he fought Dumas, the Tour doctor, claiming he'd been drugged against his will.

Bidot believes his rider.

Malléjac – today of sound mind and body – and de Bruyne are joined by two of the Bretons, Pardoën and Morvan, as well as Jempy Schmitz, the man Roger Hassenforder calls the camel due to his hunched back.

The question is – as the riders pass through the Flemish Ardennes – how far does Darrigade let the breakaway get? At one point, it's 6'30", which is when Darrigade yells at his teammates Forestier and Mahé to do some work off the front. Even the Italians are putting in a shift.

Few Italians ever make it to this part of the world where Classics are contested by a field made up of 90% Belgian riders. Too grey, too dark, too... northern. But watching Fantini, Nencini, De Filippis, and even the invisible man Fornara, you'd think they were regulars, as the bumps shake the peloton to life.

Darrigade is getting a ride home. The gap is coming down steadily with Malléjac putting the brakes on the breakaway and the combination of France and Italy putting their collective hammers down at the front of the chasing peloton. A classic stage in Classics country, then. André may even have hopes of a stage win.

The border, when it comes, is open and the riders are waved through by border guards and customs officials of both colours. The bare, pot-holed roads of Belgium are immediately replaced by lines of poplars, smooth American-financed tarmac and the reassuring hum of wheels on pliant ground. There are nods and satisfied noises among the 80 or so riders now swooping on De Bruyne, Malléjac and the rest.

WALKO

A moment of reflection

And – for those of a romantic disposition – a moment of reflection.

It is at precisely this point, carefully orchestrated by the organisers, that the Tour passes the milestone of 200,000km. Battle-worn old journalist Gaston Bénac, today in a 2CV that has taken a battering on the shelled-out roads of Belgium, breathes a sigh and raises an imaginary glass to the men of Tours gone by.

To Eugène Christophe and his broken forks, to Rene Vietto and his sacrifice. To Coppi, Bartali, Bobet… ahhh, 200,000km dear boy, he turns to André Chassaignon. 200,000km, dear boy.

200,001km now, old man, retorts Chassaignon, notebook poised at the ready, wry smile on his face.

De Bruyne takes one last look over his shoulder. The team cars have pulled out, which means the peloton is closing, but these roads are familiar. They lead to the velodrome. There's a last patch of cobbles – easy ones – and Malléjac's feet are stiff. De Bruyne knows that's a sign of tiredness and puts in one final effort to beat off his man. Pardoën and Schmitz attack Malléjac, which brings one last thrashing of the pedals from the Breton. De Bruyne enters the velodrome, which is full of Belgians, of course it is, it's always full of Belgians. A roar erupts; he takes the first bank and Pardoën is closing in. Down the straight, he takes the racing line to the next bank and looks over his right shoulder. No one there.

The battle is for second place.

De Bruyne lifts his arms aloft, and in doing so, catches a glimpse of the peloton rounding the first bank. It's another win. He could get used to this.

Belgium Attacks, Bidot Worries

The Broom Wagon

A single vehicle stalks our riders every day. Once the peloton and its stragglers have gone, the team cars and the police have waved their last to the assembled crowds, two merry men in a van, carrying a symbolic broom, bring up the rear. Behind them, a trailer for bikes that have been abandoned by riders who have themselves abandoned the Tour.

It isn't long into this stage that Hans Hollenstein, the young Swiss rider, decides to end his own Tour. He's been struggling with something, he's not sure what and if we're to be honest, it's hard to say what he's struggling with. Morale, maybe.

He makes a sign as if to say he has an injury, somewhere on this leg, or maybe that leg. The drivers of the broom wagon ask no questions; not their place. Just give us the bike, step in here, sunshine, take a seat. Do you need a doctor? No? The bike hangs cruelly from the trailer, goading its rider.

Hollenstein has raced hard this year, with two top 10 finishes in the Swiss Tours - the Tour of Switzerland which focuses on the German side of his country, and the Tour of Romandie, which is more French. The Tour de France wasn't really on his radar and besides, Swiss cycling is entering a lull. Hollenstein knows it, his team knows it, why race too hard?

So, watching the Belgian countryside pass by through the windows, Hans Hollenstein sits alone. He wonders what might have been, had he been in the mood to race, had he been properly fit. He wonders who is next in the broom wagon. With his limited French, he overhears the driver and his friend chatting about a fall in Brussels. Hans wishes he had brought something to read. There's at least four more hours of this. He sinks his head into his hands and wishes for a more comfortable seat than this simple wooden bench.

A journey in the broom wagon is far from smooth. As the

cars concertina on the narrow Belgian roads, the wagon is forced to stop and wait, before pulling off only to stop a few seconds later. Within a few hundred metres, you're travelling at 60km per hour, chasing police cars, stopping abruptly once more. Only this time, the owners of the wagon are leaping out, alarm on their faces, panic in their voices. Be a Swiss rider, thinks Hollenstein, be a colleague. It's Fausto Luratti, indeed another Swiss, but this one is covered in blood. A bad fall indeed, a real injury this time, not morale, not a slight twinge in the knee, and Luratti thinks of Alex Burtin his Technical Director and how he'll get his team back to Paris. Not even two stages in and two men down.

They take Luratti away quicker than he arrived, Hollenstein watching helplessly as his compatriot is taken in an ambulance. Sit and watch. It's a long way to Lille, where Hollenstein faces the greatest shame of all, stepping out of the broom wagon. He has time to perfect his story.

Nine Men Stay Away For The Day
7th July 1956
Stage 3, Lille to Rouen, 294km

The Breakaway The Got Away

Yesterday, the combination of De Bruyne and Mallejac dug in deep for what, 43 seconds? Anyone tempted to break away while André Darrigade is directing the peloton knows that you need more than a handful of men, and you need more than a little luck.

Today's break is nine-strong, and includes: Mahé, Padovan, Huyghe, Barbosa, Chaussabel, Le Ber, Van der Pluym, Frei and Desmet. Something of a multi-coloured, multi-cultural breakaway if you want. French, Breton, Dutch, Belgian, Portuguese (Luxembourg, really), Swiss, North-East-Centre and South-East.

An in variety comes strength, thinks André Darrigade as he leans in to Marcel Bidot's car window and hears of the men in the break. Only the Spanish would be inclined to ride with him, and what's in it for them?

André tries to strike a deal with Lorono and Bahamontes. Will you ride, he asks. I'll lead you out, he offers. They shake their heads. Not doing it.

The breakaway of nine is applying the pressure by relaying constantly at 50km per hour. Behind, the peloton is slipping badly. Blackboards inform the break that they are 5 minutes ahead, and soon 6, soon 10. Soon they are an enormous 20 minutes ahead of the peloton and not a single man is letting the pace drop.

Darrigade's worst fears have been realised. With a rider from every team in the break, their teammates are sitting up, joking around, laughing. He glares and they laugh back. No one will work. André has missed his chance, and the yellow jersey is slipping from his back with every pedal stroke. What a shit day, he thinks, as the flat marshlands of Picardy and the Pas-de-Calais roll by in a never-ending glut of glumness, of wet greys and murky greens, and the rusty red-brick façades of Abbeville suck the life out of Darrigade and the peloton.

Three Virtual Yellow Jerseys

The mind of a bike racer is constantly shifting. There is firstly survival. Am I going to hit a pothole? Am I going to make it round this corner? Can I reach within the time limits today? Within each rider is a pessimist that needs to be controlled – or best of all – ignored.

Then there is the immediate. Am I going to be overtaken? Have I worn this man down? The immediate is all about reaction and gut feeling.

And then there is the optimist. Will I win this race? How many minutes do I have in hand? The optimist is not within every rider. There are those who doze at the back of the peloton every day, drinking sugared beer and eating more than is healthy. Their only ambition is to reach the destination before the cut-off. An optimist, however, is always jockeying for position and thinking about how to find an edge.

Three men are in the optimist phase right now. Desmet, Huyghe and Mahé have all worked out that one of them will be wearing the yellow jersey this evening, and as they relay, the virtual yellow jersey changes hands.

Gilbert Desmet

Gilbert Desmet is a young Belgian rider from Lichtervelde. Fast, and suited to the narrow, cobbled uphill finish in Rouen, Desmet is a danger. He has made his name in kermesse and criterium racing in Belgium, touring his native country from a young age with his bike and pitching up at any race that would have him. He is still young and he is still inexperienced, however.

François Mahé

That is the thought of François Mahé, a Breton riding for the French national team. He finished 10th last year, so he knows what he's doing. The man from Morbihan knows what it's like to wear yellow, which is more than can be said for his two breakaway compadres.

Camille Huyghe

Camille Huyghe has had the honour of going past his home town Auxi-le-Chateau, if not quite through it. A few banners and a handful of runners alongside him were enough to keep him in good cheer. The man from the Nord-Est-Centre team has no huge ambitions, and the thought of yellow frightens him as much as it excites him.

Huyghe is not an optimist.

Immediately, Claude Le Ber launches an attack off the front. We've hit that climb in Rouen, which is cobbled and slippy. Le Ber is large, and adept at this kind of climb. Padovan follows, the Italian perhaps not so adept at these climbs, but he knows the descent to follow is far easier. The three virtual yellow jerseys eye each other up, and Camille Huyghe turns optimist and makes his move.

Desmet and Mahé are caught in the immediate. Instinct takes over and as one they follow but Huyghe is fast. Faster than they had thought. Why did nobody tell us about this fella?

Padovan edges ahead of Huyghe as Le Ber falls away. Too big.

Huyghe edges ahead of Padovan, but suddenly drops back, beyond Le Ber, past Desmet, past Mahé and even Barbosa. He curses his luck – a flat tyre, just 1000m from the finish line, right underneath the flamme rouge. Nobody looks back, they're all caught up in the immediate as Camille Huyghe sits on the pavement and waits for his support car to turn up and replace his wheel. He's not changing anything himself today, he's done his work.

Padovan takes the victory at the line, and it's Gilbert Desmet who takes yellow, ahead of a frustrated Mahé.

Around 20 minutes later, when Desmet and Mahé have long since had a wash and something to eat, André Darrigade crosses the line, shaking his head and muttering curses at the riders who have done nothing to help him today. He'll remember them, each and every one of them.

An Alsatian Among The Bretons
8th July 1956
Stage 4a, Time Trial, Rouen, 15.1k
Stage 4b, Rouen to Caen, 125k

An Alsatian Among The Bretons

The keen observer would have noticed that Roger Hassenforder is riding for the Ouest team, which is to all intents and purposes, the Breton team. There are notable exceptions, but the general rule is that if you're from the region, you ride for the region. And that had almost always been the case. Hassenforder, being from Alsace, would usually have found a place in the Nord-Est-Centre team.

So why is he riding for the Bretons?

Or more pertinently, why is he not riding for the Nord-Est-Centre team?

The answer to that is: because he's Roger Hassenforder. A trouble-maker. An enigma wrapped in a joke wrapped in a superstar wrapped in a ticking timebomb.

Hassenforder was born in Sausheim, not far from Colmar in the Alsace region. His formative years were spent in the shadow of German occupation, which gave the young Roger plenty of opportunity for mischief. His teacher was a small, bald, frail-looking German man the children named 'Popeye'. Suspecting that Popeye was vulnerable to the occasional bribe, Roger would sneak him some of the family rations of lard, resulting in marks that were indirectly proportionate to Roger's academic aptitude.

When Popeye was replaced by a slim, younger German lady who was immune to Roger's lard, he simply replied: "She wants it really. She's just trying to watch her weight", and Roger's marks returned to normal.

For many years, Roger simply didn't bother going to school. When he did, he was caught burning petrol in the ink pots and was shown the door.

Landmines

The Germans came and went, came back again – and then left in the liberation, but left behind a number of landmines. Roger, of course, had been watching them place the landmines, and scurried over to retrieve the liquid and the detonators inside each one. Simply tap on the top with a screwdriver, and the landmine revealed its treasure to you. Perfect for fishing, so it turned out – simply detonate in the water, and the dead fish rise to the surface.

Roger survived this expedition, but one of his best friends returned from landmine-gathering without his leg.

As the occupation went on, Roger got more adventurous. There were revolvers, grenades, cigarettes and a whole host of weapons and explosives that Roger kept hidden in the tomb of an old priest Roger had a particular affection for. The Germans had long suspected him, and even caught him red-handed stealing cigarettes one day, but never found his little arsenal.

Roger particularly liked a swing-barrel revolver that he found on one of his expeditions into enemy territory. The revolver failed to fire when Roger pulled the trigger, aiming carelessly at a tree. He pulled again, but once more, the revolver failed. He pointed it as his sister and then at his grand-mother, both of whom ran away screaming.

It was only later that day, when the revolver was in Roger's pocket that it finally fired. The bullet penetrated Roger's hand, blood flowed down his leg. It was a fall, he told his mother. Some raised ironworks, quite a bad cut. His father only found out what happened two days later, and ordered him to go to hospital.

With the Germans still occupying Sausheim, the only way to get to the hospital in Mulhouse was through the forest, hoping the Germans wouldn't see him. Carrying a white flag, Roger stumbled head-down through the trees. German voices called out, gunshots were fired, bullets whistled past Roger's ears. Finally, Roger was caught by a German officer and beaten severely, before being told to go to Colmar hospital instead.

Returning home, Roger takes his mother's bike and so begins his love of cycling. Or, to be more precise at this stage in his cycling career, cyclo-cross. Riding through the mud and the bomb craters with one good hand, one bad, Roger reaches Colmar hospital to find the war-wounded naturally given preference over a boy with a bullet in his hand.

By 4am, a delirious Roger is singing La Marseillaise while a German surgeon removes the bullet. He is ordered to stay in the hospital.

Christmas

As you're beginning to get an impression of the type of boy Roger Hassenforder was, you can probably imagine that Roger was not the type to take orders. With fighting raging around the hospital, Roger was forced to stay put.

Finally, with Christmas approaching, he escaped the hospital through the kitchen window, searched for his mother's bike in vain and ran into the town square, finding another bike. He ripped the bag off the handlebars and rode the 40km back to Sausheim to find that the fighting had spread to his home town. It would have been an apocalyptic scene as Roger approached Sausheim; the flames would have been visible from miles away. The family home had not been spared, and Mrs Hassenforder was hiding at a neighbours house.

On spotting him, she did a double-take. Who was this fat-faced child staring through the window? Roger had been gone for six weeks and had gained 10 kilos in the process.

Come summer, and with the Germans out of the way, Roger went back to the priest's tomb to discover that his small arsenal had been left untouched. Bingo. Time to have some fun.

There was a small temporary toilet in the forest, miraculously untouched by the retreating army. Roger moved his arsenal to the toilet in the forest and promised his friends a fireworks show. Over several days, he continued to douse the toilet with petrol and sulphates until finally, with invites sent, Roger was ready to detonate the stolen loot.

With his friends hiding behind an embankment, Roger lit the fuse and jumped on his bike. The explosion was ferocious; reports stated that the noise could be heard over ten kilometres away. Roger was found 20 metres from his bike, his clothes and his skin charred black by the fire. At first, the pain didn't even occur to him. His friends gawped, stupefied at the figure standing before them. And then a scream. The pain seared from toenail to scalp and back again, and Roger ran. He ran, hoping to outpace the pain, back to his mother. Back to the hospital in Mulhouse where he would spend the next 6 months suffering skin grafts and painkillers and crutches.

And the discovery, later that summer, that some of the more

potent explosives had failed to detonate. Had they succeeded, there would surely have been no Roger Hassenforder at the 1956 Tour de France.

Just One Year Ago…

Throughout his career as a cyclist, Roger Hassenforder would prove no less explosive. He rode mainly for himself, abandoning when he had had enough, attacking when he felt like it, and wasting his energy to the detriment of his teammates.

In 1955, Hassenforder was selected for Saveur Ducazeaux's North-East-Centre team alongside Gilbert Bauvin. After participating in the breakaway in the first stage, he took it upon himself to attempt to bridge the gap in the second stage. Bauvin was furious at the Alsacien for wasting his energy and that of his teammates.

"Watch my back wheel tomorrow, Bauvin," he yelled at the dinner table. "I'll be done with my massage by the time you finish."

The next morning, it was Louison Bobet who broke away at the very start of the stage. Having spent his early career fomenting a venomous rivalry with "Bobette", it was highly unlikely Hassenforder would go with him. But go with him he did, and the two put aside their differences to force a pace that the peloton would find too much to bear.

Hassenforder lost his bidons at a railway crossing, which meant he had to accept whatever he could from the crowds lining the road. 20 kilometres from the finish in Roubaix, Roger felt so good that he hit the bottom of a short but steep hill alone, only to reach the top having been hit with the hammer. He finished back in 12th, but more importantly, Gilbert Bauvin finished a whole 30 minutes behind.

That night at the dinner table, only Roger Walkowiak and Gilbert Scodeller would talk to him. The rest of the team had already shunned Hassenforder for his alliance with Bobet and the manner with which he had forced the pace all day.

Roger's attitude was more of a serene "screw them", promising to give his teammates another thrashing the next day on the stage from Metz to Colmar. And he was indeed true to his word, forming the early breakaway and then insisting that the pace of the breakaway was too slow, charging ahead and taking with him a handful of men. Some refused to ride with him. Jean Bobet, brother of Louison, declined to work on the front – his teammate was in yellow, and his job was to slow things down. But alone, Hassenforder won the stage, entering his home velodrome of Colmar with 9 minutes ahead of the peloton.

Roger Hassenforder was 2nd in the Tour de France.

Colmar expoded with joy. Parties went on well into the night, and Roger was naturally the life and soul of Colmar that evening.

However, in the North-East-Centre team, the fractures were widening. They blamed him for taking Jean Bobet higher up the general classification with him. They blamed him for riding against Gilbert Bauvin. And they were right – he was riding against Bauvin. He was riding against all 9 teammates, and even his technical director Ducazeaux declared "we are 9 now."

All this, of course, despite Roger Hassenforder regularly filling the communal coffers.

On the stage from Colmar to Zurich, Roger was beginning to feel the strain of the previous day's efforts. He was shunned not just by his teammates, but by the whole peloton. Not a soul spoke to Hassenforder, whose rumbustious behaviour hid a sensitive soul for whom isolation is punishment. He had no allies, and little by little, kilometre by kilometre, the heart went out of Hassen's tour.

In the 8th stage, from Thonon-les-Bains to Briancon, Roger immediately falls out of the back of the peloton and stops at the side of the road.

"Get me the doctor. I've got ulcers in my mouth."

Marius Dupin, race commissioner, eyes Hassenforder with suspicion: "Doctor, is he really ill?"

Dr Dumas takes one look at the fallen rider and says,

"As a man, I'd have to say he's taking the piss out of us all. As a doctor, I'd have to concur that he does have ulcers."

And so ended Roger Hassenforder's tumultuous Tour of 1955. Isolated by the peloton, adored and despised by the fans in equal measure, and eventually poorer for the lack of post-Tour contracts, Roger Hassenforder locked his bike away and returned to his true passion: hunting. He would speak of 1956 and his desire to return to the Tour, but not under the tutelage of Sauveur Ducazeaux, and especially not alongside that rat Gilbert Bauvin.

Perhaps being ostracised from his regional team had a mollifying effect on Hassenforder. With the help of team director Francis Pelissier, the Alsacien discovered a lighter, more race-ready diet. More liquid, less fat. Shorter training rides, more discipline.

Rebuilding His Reputation

Roger had returned to riding in 1956 with the aim of rebuilding his reputation both with the fans and his peers in the peloton. The financial difficulties he suffered at the end of 1955 were – perhaps – the final straw for a man whose impetuous behaviour had nearly ruined him. After all, how could he hunt elephants in Cameroon on the pittance he earned from last season?

The problem remained, however. None of the Technical Directors of the Tour teams would take on Hassenforder after last year's antics. For Ducazeaux, it was a flat "non". But fate would have mercy on Roger. Albert Bouvet, one of the first names on Leon Le Calvez's Ouest teamsheet, pulled out of the Tour due to a knee injury. Le Calvez turned to Roger Hassenforder.

"I'm a little bit Breton", he joked to reporters. "Why, my grandmother used to play the bagpipes."

Under Le Calvez, Roger Hassenforder had found a new lease of life. In stage 1, Roger was frequently at the front of the peloton trying to reduce Andre Darrigade's lead. He led the counter-attack on the second stage, successfully pegging back the breakaway of Debruyne, Mallejac and Pardoen.

And so, here at the fourth stage, fate is ready to pounce on Roger Hassenforder once more.

The Broken Pedal

Today's stage is broken up into two parts. Firstly, and very early in the morning, a time trial around the Essarts circuit.

Not Roger's favourite discipline, and certainly not a time trial that would suit him. This would be an opportunity for Gaul, Brankart, Bahamontes and Geminiani – the climbers will have a chance to earn back some of the significant losses they have incurred over the first few stages.

Roger's aim is simply to get through the morning.

However, just a few hundred metres into Roger's effort, a pedal breaks. Instantly, he's off his bike, fiddling with the pedal, trying to fix it back, but there's no way Roger can ride like this.

"What am I meant to do?" he pleads with the race

commissioner.

"Take your bike back – you can't replace it during a time trial. Go ask Felix for the rule book."

Is this it, he wonders. Is this the end of my Tour? Unable to complete a time trial, unable to complete a stage because of a broken pedal?

"No Hassen," Felix reassures him. "You'll just have to take the time of the last man over the line."

"Is that all? That's brilliant!" beams Roger.

"Plus 5%, of course. As a penalty."

He shrugs. He really doesn't care.

The first men are returning to the tents prepared for the riders who have to face the 125km from Rouen to Caen in the afternoon. The effort has visibly put a strain on some riders, especially the rouleurs and the support men not used to tackling such steep hills so early in a tour. One by one, they drape themselves over armchairs, stuff their mouths with breakfast and for some – sleep.

The new Roger Hassenforder, the 1956 model, is having none of this. For Roger, it's an opportunity to take his revenge on fate. A fresh rider – with a proper warm-up – would be no contest for the time-trial-weary peloton. So while the other riders are draped over chaise longues, some sleeping, others reading or being massaged by their soigneurs, Roger Hassenforder is out on the course warming up.

Just 40km into the 125km stage from Rouen to Caen, Roger makes his move, and it's his teammates Amande Audaire and Fernand Picot, along with Barbotin and Privat from the French national team, followed by Voorting and Close, who follow in his wake.

Just one year ago, Hassenforder was without friends and had been shunned by his teammates who refused to talk to him. Today, he is the captain of a group of three Bretons, both of whom are putting in hard turns on the front for Hassen. What has happened behind is a fracturing of the peloton. Walkowiak, Wagtmans and Bauvin are part of a group of five behind, with the Italian Nencini and Hassenforder's teammate and mentor Louis Caput.

Further back, there's a Darrigade group which is the only group not to include a Breton. Darrigade knows that behind him, the yellow jersey of Desmet is struggling. He latches onto the team car and enquires about the gap between his group and the peloton. The car drops back and makes enquiries over the radio, before pulling back in. Darrigade leans in, and from his demeanour, it is obvious that the yellow jersey is back in play.

At the front, Hassenforder's advantage is growing. His teammates Audaire and Picot are hunched over their handlebars, gritting their teeth. The French riders are clinging on, and at times even pull from the front as well. The kilometres tick down and the two chasing groups come together, mostly through Darrigade's insistence.

It is inevitable, then, that Roger Hassenforder wins this stage, in what was not so much a sprint as a coronation. His teammates have given their all for Hassen, and they are richly rewarded as the Ouest team take the lead in the team classification, also known as the Martini challenge. That means more money in the Breton coffers.

And so, as André Darrigade pulls on the yellow jersey with Gilbert Desmet finishing over 15 minutes behind, the man from Narrosse is almost a footnote. He still hopes, of course, that he can hold the jersey until the Pyrenees and beyond, which is a stretch given that there isn't a single member of his team who doesn't hope to steal the jersey from his back.

The cheers are not for Darrigade. They are entirely for Roger Hassenforder – popular once more.

Brittany First
9th July 1956
Caen to Saint-Malo, 189km

The Doctor Calls

We are just four stages into this Tour de France, and the Tour physician, Dr. Dumas, has hardly slept. First of all, Fritz Schär, the Swiss ratagasse, is suffering from his injuries after a fall yesterday. An innocent slip at the time, no more than that, but Schär landed on his brakes. A contortionist's fall, but one that has led to him spitting blood this morning and Dr. Dumas has told him he can continue – but at the risk of several weeks' suffering.

"Speak slowly," insists Schär. "I understand French, but only if you speak slowly."

Dr. Dumas does his best, but the doctor's habit of machine-gun diagnosis takes over, and Schär understands the meaning, if not the words. His Tour is over.

Nello Laurédi is next in the Doctor's waiting room. He has been coughing since the start of the Tour, but not at the expense of speed. He finds himself third in the General Classification, so Dr. Dumas is wondering why he has been visited.

"But I also have a pain, just here," says Laurédi, pointing at his heart.

Dr. Dumas studies the electrocardiogram taken in Reims ahead of the Tour. "There's nothing wrong with you. And you've been riding rather well, have you not?"

Dr. Dumas doesn't care for cycling. He'd rather be walking in the Pyrenees, but he makes more money doing the Tour than he makes all year. He is making an effort.

"Come to think of it," muses the third-placed rider, "I took this tonic in Italy during the Giro. My cough stopped after the Giro when I stopped taking it."

Dumas has heard this one before. "You're using it again, aren't you."

"Yes, Doctor."

He nods. "You know what to do."

Next.

Jean Dotto is next, although Dotto is made of tough stuff. He fell on yesterday's stage, hurting his head.

"Please, no bandages this year, Doctor. It's hot out there."

Dumas is pleased. This one's simple. In fact, as it turns out, only the Belgians and the Italians have failed to take advantage of the Doctor's services, and he's beginning to wonder how the likes of Brankart are getting by without him.

Brankart, he knows, is suffering from a knee injury, and Dr. Dumas, having taken a slight interest in the event this year, knows that the Belgian rider has been losing time even to his own teammates, and all this after he finished 2nd in the Tour last year. Falling ten minutes behind Stan Ockers is embarrassing for someone like Brankart, so much so that on today's stage from Caen to Saint Malo, Brankart is supposed to play the part of the faithful lieutenant to Ockers. He's having none of it, refusing to drop back for water.

Brittany First

Gégène Serves The Drinks

As we travel from Normandy to Brittany, the Breton riders are in good heart. Yesterday's escapade saw Roger Hassenforder take the green jersey, and his teammate Eugène Letendre spent the morning passing Calvados around the peloton. A stimulant perhaps not recommended by the Doctor himself, but the Ouest team's resident Norman is not passing up his moment in the sunshine. Vous êtes chez moi he proffers. Drink.

Nicknamed Gégène, Letendre is a stocky, round-faced rider making his Tour debut. He's a country boy. His only dalliance with the big city was a few minutes at the Gare Saint-Lazare, before – so he says – returning back to Normandy from whence he came. Eugène is a cyclist by necessity as much as talent. When his father died, Eugène felt a certain responsibility to provide for his family – his mother and his three brothers, who all lived together in relative poverty.

He watched bike races on Sundays and thought to himself – they're earning a pretty packet. I can do that. And he did, using his savings to buy a rusty race bike with one pedal. He swung a lamp over the front of his bike and trained until late at night after work. Every bike race was for his family, every penny he earned went towards filling the soup pot at night and buying bread in the morning.

His one victory to date was in Bobet country – Brittany. With one lap to go before the finish, Gégène was exhausted. At the time, he was doing military service, and had slept little. He hid behind a bale of hay, took some rest, and rode out to discover that he was the first man to cross the line. Everyone else was still on that last lap.

But Letendre could not take the prize that day. He was too much of a good man to let everyone think he had won fairly.

And that's Gégène all over – a good man. A man who looks after others. The perfect teammate, in other words. And for anyone who thought that handing out some Calvados was his way of knocking the peloton out ahead of a long slog into Brittany, they had misread the man.

Vous êtes chez moi, he says, et j'en suis fier.

And I'm proud to have you here.

Joseph's Ride Home

There is, for once, no rush. The riders are rolling through the slightly fermented Normandy countryside at a modest 38km/h. Normandy is cycling country, if you really love cycling. The Bretons might lay their claim, but Normandy is rolling hills, with long, quiet roads, sharp climbs and steep drops, before ironing itself out into false flats among low hedgerows. The weather may not play ball, but Normandy is a region where cycling is taken seriously, and very often, is taken slower in order to take in the view.

And the odour of rotting apples, which is pleasing. In a way.

The majority of this stage takes place in Normandy, in fact. It's only after Avranches that the softer-sounding Normandy village names turn into slightly stranger Breton towns such as Baguer-Pican. It's before Avranches that the breakaway forms. Nolten and Bertolo think they could make a day of it before they're joined by Walkowiak, Fantini, Morvan (a Breton), and a few others.

Behind, Darrigade keeps an eye on the blackboards, making sure not to let this one get too far ahead. He marshalls the troops, and even sends Forestier up ahead to join them, if he can. Put the brakes on.

Forestier is young, but wily. He sees the French team car pulling out from the group of cars ahead, and drafts behind.

Brittany First

Marcel Bidot looks in his rear view mirror and slows slightly to let Forestier catch his slipstream. The two men nod at each other.

Almost immediately, Felix Lévitan pulls out of the group of cars and speeds up alongside Bidot.

"Nice work, Marcel," he shouts. "But a little bit… obvious?"

Yellow cap pulled over his face, Bidot pulls the most gallic of gallic shrugs. What? Me? What do you mean? Oh, the rider behind? I had not seen him!

"You can tell your rider he's got a 1,000 franc fine when he arrives," screams Lévitan over the noise of their engines.

Knobhead, thinks Bidot, as he withdraws back into his 203.

The break has entered Brittany and shows no signs of slowing up. Joseph Morvan has been putting the pressure on the other riders. The man from Morbihan is a Breton thoroughbred. Wider than other riders, Morvan was brought up on the farm. His girth has been earned not through excessive crêpe-eating and cider drinking, but hard labour.

1956 has been a good year for Morvan. He has won multiple regional competitions, as well as Paris-Bourges and Rennes-Potivy. As he passes under the flamme rouge, he senses another big win is coming his way. What's more, he knows that the velodrome at which this stages finishes is an ash velodrome. Overtaking is fiendishly difficult, so if you can enter it first, you've won. Nobody else seems to know this.

It's not hard, reading the road book. Many riders take a casual glance and look for climbs, descents, feeding stations, any areas of difficulty. Few take the initiative to look at the nature of the finish line. They just think it's the same every time. Ash makes you keep your line, makes you stick to it.

And that's just what Morvan does as he enters the velodrome. Fantini, the Italian, has mysteriously appeared behind him, as well as de Groot, the Dutchman. But Morvan knows, as does every Breton, that he won't be overtaken, and he's beaming as he takes the first bend. He's laughing as he takes the second, and he's punching the air before he reaches the finish line, chest out, screaming with every ounce of his soul.

This is my stage, this is my land, this is my day.

Joseph Morvan puts Brittany first, and the night has only just begun.

The Yellow Jersey, The Level Crossing, and the Invisible Man
10th July, 1956
Saint Malo to Lorient, 192km

Monsieur Allard's Slight Miscalculation

Monsieur Allard has had a quiet Tour thus far. The Head of the Tour de France organising committee received a visit last night from the Spanish team director who complained vigorously about the St. Malo velodrome, which he claimed was responsible for several injuries in his team notably Miguel Poblet who took a heavy fall on the ash.

He shrugs quietly at Senor Esteve and smiles. "Sir, if your men can't handle a few cinders, what hope do they have of finishing this Tour? You may as well ride down to Bordeaux, cross the border and go home."

The Spaniards have returned, tails between legs, to the peloton where they belong. Monsieur Allard has other worries.

One of the responsibilities of the organising committee is to ensure that the Tour aligns itself with train timetables. To ensure that the riders are able to cross through Vicomté-sur-Rance, Monsieur Allard has recommended that the riders depart 10 minutes early. Why, who would want to disturb those hard-working people at the SNCF who have far more complex timetables to manage?

Today's breakaway is a yellow jersey breakaway. In this most frantic of Tours, it's perhaps not a surprise to see André Darrigade pulling hard at the front alongside Frei, Lampre and Impanis. After just 18km, the three have taken a minute on the peloton who have barely registered the breakaway at all. They just let them go with a sigh.

The riders have approached Vicomté-sur-Rance at speed, but are alarmed to hear the clanging of bells and see the barriers starting to fall. Darrigade charges ahead, the others in hot pursuit, and they make it across the barriers in time – just.

Monsieur Allard, following behind in a 203, is horrified. This wasn't meant to happen. He leaps out of the vehicle and runs up the control tower.

"What the hell is this? We brought the stage forward ten minutes so we'd avoid this train!"

The guard stares open-mouthed at the intruder.

"But... but... we put the trains back ten minutes for the Tour!"

Allard has lost the power of speech. Not once did he think to consult the SNCF about his decision to bring forward the départ this morning. Not once did the SNCF think to consult him about their decision to move train times back.

The peloton arrives a minute later to witness the train passing, and it's an opportunity for photographers and fans alike to get a glimpse of their favourite riders. Monsieur Allard is berated by the French team as he sits, head in hands, at the side of the road, wondering just what he's done to deserve this, and just how many more level crossings he has misjudged on the route to Lorient.

In all, the peloton has lost a further 25 seconds to the Darrigade breakaway, and more if you count the time it takes them to get back to full speed.

The Yellow Jersey, The Level Crossing, and the Invisible Man

The Reaction

Perhaps it took Monsieur Allard's oversight to shake the peloton into some kind of reaction. You may argue that were it not for the level crossing, then the Darrigade breakaway might have achieved more than just a minute and twenty-five seconds. Almost immediately, riders started putting in Darrigade levels of effort. Brankart's frame breaks as they ride through Dinan. François Mahé punctures and several other riders make silly mistakes and cause minor crashes in their pursuit of Darrigade and his hangers-on.

The riders barely have time to admire the viaduct over the Rance. Shame.

The trouble with Brittany is that the scenery can trick you. One minute you're riding on wide coastal roads, with the wind at your side knocking you inland, the next you're riding up narrow roads lined with high hedges, bracken knocking you in the face if you're not careful. Darrigade and company have negotiated this with ease, but a peloton of nearly 100 riders is taken by surprise. Even the Bretons.

Someone at the front cuts across and there's a clash of wheels. It's not just a few riders who take a fall, it's most of the peloton. In seconds, riders are down and riders are up, hauling their bikes to the side of the road. Team cars are beeping, mechanics leaping out of moving cars trying to find their riders. Him, not that one – sort him out first. You – your wheel.

It's chaos. And André Leducq is loving it. He turns to Gaston Bénac, his back-seat companion in the Miroir des Sports car.

"Ah you see, THIS is the Tour de France!"

Bénac nods in appreciation, before realising that lunch has been delayed a further ten minutes because of this hold-up.

"Driver, step on it – through the middle," he yells, as riders are cast aside for the journalists' 203. There is a certain code de la route which states that the middle of the road is no-man's land. The right-hand side is for the technical directors and their teams. The left is for the mechanics. The middle is purely for overtaking as and when required. Not for Gaston Bénac's lunch.

The Coming Together

The other thing a rider must know about Brittany, aside from the confusion of hedges and narrow roads, is that the weather can change at the drop of a hat. One minute, the riders are threatened by heavy, grey clouds, and then next, by the time the breakaway reaches Duguesclin, the sun breaks out and the town is bathed in a yellowy ochre that seems to celebrate the yellow jersey. A premonition of a Darrigade victory?

There are movements behind to put paid to that premonition. The Bretons are having none of this. Caput, Le Ber and Audaire have taken two tricolores, Lily Bergaud and René Privat with them. Fred De Bruyne doesn't want to miss out, either. Behind them, Roger Walkowiak leads a group of 7 which includes 2 further Bretons, Picot and Thomin.

The first group has caught up with the Darrigade group, who assure them that there will be no letting up in terms of pace. The second group have them in sights and within a handful of kilometres, font la jonction, as the locals say, and reform a mini peloton. There's still 100km to go, and most of Brittany to cross.

Darrigade punctures, but Bergaud is on hand to give him his spare wheel, and Bergaud sits by the roadside and waits for the team car to catch up. His duty is done, and the yellow jersey leaps back into action and wastes no time in catching the mini peloton, minus his teammate.

For the rest of the stage, then, there is a tacit agreement that the winner will come from this group. No more attacks, no more silly breaks, we'll decide who wins at the velodrome. The Bretons are confident and act effectively as Tour guides for their compatriots, who need no introduction to Brittany, but take it in good humour, allowing the various Ouest riders their opportunity to ride through their home towns ahead of the pack to soak up some Breton adulation.

The truce is broken 18km from the finish in Lorien when Le Ber decides that he's going to make a break for it. His attack fizzles out, but the riders are on edge as they approach Lorient. I thought we had a deal, yells De Bruyne, as he and Impanis attempt an attack. "Idiots," he shouts at the Bretons, who respond in kind by attacking him.

Lorient is awash with Breton flags and Breton pride, crowds ten deep lining the streets. The velodrome is a sea of black and white stripes – surely a Breton winner, they think. A choice of four, three if you discount Le Ber who bust a flush too early, not that they know that. Thomin, they think – it's Thomin the country boy – allez Jo-Jo they shout as one.

But it's Fred De Bruyne who nicks it on the line, and the Bretons' run of luck comes to an end. André Darrigade doesn't participate in the sprint, he knows his yellow jersey is safe, with blackboards putting the peloton at 11 minutes back.

And quietly, in the pack, a certain Roger Walkowiak takes the same time as the Belgian sprinter and the yellow jersey. Nobody pays any attention to the man in the violet jersey, with his innocent face, rosy cheeks and wiry hair. And nobody notices, when they read the General Classification that evening, that Roger Walkowiak is now 5th in the Tour de France. They skip over his name because a) it's hard to pronounce and b) they know it won't be there for much longer. It is quite possible that Roger Walkowiak, the Invisible Man, agrees with them.

But they're just thinking of Darrigade, and how easy he made it all look, and André himself is thinking of holding on to yellow through the Pyrenees and maybe over the Alps. At least, with a succession of flat stages before Luchon, André will be able to wear his yellow jersey as the Tour passes through his home town of Narrosse. And beyond that? Perhaps, he thinks. Just perhaps he could win the Tour. Your sprinter-routier has ambitions…

The Water Carrier, the Saviour, and the Protector
11th July 1956
Lorient to Angers, 242km

Dreams of Yellow

Has any Tour been approached at such a furious pace? The riders, heading east into the Loire valley today, may be forgiven for taking today's stage at a slightly slower speed. The sun is shining, there's barely a hint of a breeze, the mercury is rising. The road to Angers lies ahead and André Darrigade dreams of wearing yellow in front of friends and family when the caravan reaches Bordeaux in a few days' time.

Roger Walkowiak has no such hopes. A regular in chasing groups in between peloton and breakaway, the man from Montluçon appears never to carry any particular aspirations. Walkowiak is smaller than most riders. His round cheeks, wiry hair and unassuming stare make him the perfect breakaway companion – generally not noticed by others. The avid reader may have noticed his name in various breakaways, but Walkowiak rides for others, not for himself.

A mention in L'Equipe or Miroir des Sports is as good as it gets for the water-carrier. For Walkowiak, a day spent shuttling between riders with bidons full of water or sugared beer is de rigueur.

Usually.

And so, when the peloton fractures early in this stage to the Loire Valley, Roger Walkowiak's presence in the second of three groups is taken at face value. He's not trying to win, so just why is he riding so prominently? Indeed, when the front two groups join to form what is possibly the Tour's largest breakaway yet, nobody questions Walkowiak's presence. Together, these twenty-plus men set about putting a gap between themselves and their chasers, and our angel-faced Walkowiak is putting in the hard shifts.

By the time the peloton reaches Hérac, the gap has reached nearly 5 minutes and is growing. Some day for lounging around on bikes in the sunshine – the lead group went through town a full 30 minutes ahead of schedule. The locals, thankfully, were forewarned.

Darrigade's Nightmare Scenario

On any other day, that would be that. André Darrigade would be leading the chase, pulling the peloton back to within breathing distance of the breakaway, ably supported by his tricolore teammates. But today is fast becoming far from normal.

For André Darrigade, the nightmare is just beginning.

It takes twenty men to chase down a breakaway of this size. Twenty men taking shifts on the front and putting in maximum effort – that will keep the pace up to around 50km/h.

The Belgians are not helping. They're looking after Ockers and Brankart who have mountains aspirations, and both are eyeing up Gaul who is tucked safely behind them. A pleasant checkmate. The Italians have got Fantini up at the front. They're not going to chase down one of their own.

The French themselves are torn. Gilbert Bauvin is in the breakaway, but the aim at the start of the day was to keep Darrigade in yellow. For the time being, there's no reason to believe that he won't keep his jersey. However, without the support of competing nations, there's a risk that the gap will grow, and Bauvin might gain some time ahead of the mountains.

Perhaps they should start defending Gilbert instead?

Darrigade is hitting the front in vain. The gap levels out for a while, but almost as one, Darrigade included, the peloton gives up. Waves the white flag. And that gap grows to ten minutes, fifteen minutes, twenty minutes. There's nothing left in the tank. Marcel Bidot pulls up alongside in the white 203 and yells his encouragement at the yellow jersey, but Darrigade feels it slipping away and shakes his head, sweat flicking Bidot in the face.

"No one's riding for us, Marcel. Forget it."

"Keep the gap down, André," he insists. "You can hang on to the jersey. Stay focused."

Virtual Yellow

At the front, the blackboards relay the size of the gap. Every few kilometres, the board is taken down, wiped furiously and the number increases. 25 minutes. The wily Gilbert Bauvin – usually a teammate of Walkowiak's in the Nord-Est-Centre team – realises faster than anyone else and draws up alongside.

"Yellow jersey, eh Roger?" he winks.

"Huh?"

"You're virtual yellow. Have you not been looking at the gaps?"

He had not.

The man with no aspirations, the man with no hope had not

been reading the blackboards and had not been monitoring the gap at all. All of a sudden, under the beating sun in the Loire valley, Roger Walkowiak is riding into first place of the Tour. Dousing himself with water, he realises that Sauveur Ducazeaux is alongside in the Nord-Est-Centre team car, eyes closed in the passenger seat, a picture of calm.

And perhaps a smile playing on that undulating face of his?

With the realisation that he would be leading the Tour, Roger Walkowiak runs through the scenarios of how he might not become leader. He might puncture. But even then, the team car is nearby and punctures are quick to repair this year. Change a wheel. Scodeller is up there too, so a teammate can even offer his wheel. He might veer off the side of the road. Injure himself. But he's ridden over a thousand kilometres without much incident. Why would that happen now?

He thinks of Sauveur Ducazeaux. How could he stay so calm? How can he sleep? Sauveur my saviour, he thinks.

Even in the velodrome at Angers, no one seems to be aware that Roger Walkowiak is the virtual leader. He crosses the line with a few backslaps from his breakaway colleagues – Bauvin included. Fantini appears to have won, he's already on his victory lap, arms thrust in the air.

The Long Wait

Roger sits and watches the chronometer. It's true what they say. Time does slow down when you're watching the clock. He pre-consoles himself with the thought of Darrigade coming through the entrance of the velodrome, staying in yellow, but with himself just a minute behind. The man with no ambition is slowly discovering what it's like to win.

19 minutes, and still no Darrigade. He fixes his eyes on the clock and to distract himself, looks away towards the entrance.

No riders. Not even the crowd noise from an oncoming peloton. How could they be so far behind? He gets up and tears start falling from his eyes. Not many, but enough for team director Ducazeaux to notice.

"I said you could ride a big one," he says, pulling Walkowiak towards him.

"What do I do now?"

"Well, like the rest of us. You keep watching and waiting for Darrigade, and then you go up on stage to collect your jersey. Compose yourself, son. It's not as if you don't deserve it."

You'll Have To Lose That Jersey

That evening, Roger Walkowiak looked at himself in the mirror in his hotel bedroom. Alone with the yellow jersey for the first time in his life, he pulled it on for the second time that day and studied himself. It's not so unusual, he thought. It's not so out of place. And if I can keep it a few stages, Pierrette will be there in Bordeaux to welcome me. If I'm wearing yellow then, she'll be ever so proud. We can spend the rest day together.

Pierrette is everything to Roger.

Roger hadn't noticed Ducazeaux at the door.

"You'll have to lose that jersey, Roger", he pronounced in a solemn tone, as if he'd been preparing this speech.

And, indeed, he had.

"Huh? What?"

"That jersey. You can't keep it."

"But I've only just got it Sauveur! I can't give it up now."

"Give it up you shall," replied Ducazeaux, sitting his protégé down on the bed. "And listen… because this is what we're going to do. You're a target now. Every man in the peloton will recognise that you're a danger. You went toe-to-toe with

Bobet in the mountains at the Dauphiné, do you think they won't remember that? Do you think they don't see you as a danger? You have a target on your back and they won't let you in any breakaways. You're not going to win the Tour carrying the jersey all the way to Paris. It doesn't work like that."

"But…" blubbed Walkowiak.

"No buts. You have to give it up. We'll get it back later. I have a plan"

"But I want to wear it into Bordeaux. So Pierrette can see me in yellow. It's all she'll ever have wanted. She'll be there at the velodrome, she's holidaying there. Please, Sauveur. Please, sir."

"Bordeaux," repeated Ducazeaux, pensively.

"It's just two stages. Please, I beg you."

Those cow eyes. It's like dealing with a puppy, not a bike rider.

"Very well," sighed Ducazeaux. "Very well. Bordeaux it is."

Later that evening, Ducazeaux sat down with Adolphe Deledda to firm out his plans. Deledda was a veteran of the Tour – he'd ridden alongside Bobet and Geminiani and had carried water himself for the best of the tricolores. A step back to regional teams was inevitable given his age, but Deledda now had a major – and unexpected – role to play.

"He wants to keep the jersey until Bordeaux, Adolphe."

Deledda looked stunned. "Is he mad?"

"Quite possibly. But you know, having the yellow jersey can do strange things to a man. I need your help."

"Always, sir."

"Protect him until Bordeaux. Then make sure that he loses the jersey after the rest day. Not too much time, but make it retrievable. Five minutes will do. We'll chip away in the mountains. The climbers like Gaul and Bahamontes are too far out to make any sort of difference now. You'll then pull him through on the flat stages back to Paris. I actually think we can win this Tour, Adolphe. I really do."

Deledda nodded. Ducazeaux might be mad, but it wasn't unreasonable.

The only problem might be convincing Roger Walkowiak that he could win the Tour.

Why do they have to go so fast?
12th July 1956
Stage 8, Angers to La Rochelle, 180km

The Good Old Days

There are those around le Tour who miss those days where the riders would roll along at 30km per hour. Andre Leducq, French legend and multiple Tour winner, is one such man.

Why do they have to go so quickly? Why can't they enjoy the scenery?

Leducq is one of many journalists who have gone ahead to the 20km mark in Saint-Lambert-du-Lattay where the winegrowers of the region are lining the roads for some widely advertised degustation – wine-tasting. Coteaux de Layon makes some of the finest sweet wine in all of France, what an opportunity not to miss out on. The old men of Tours gone past can gather here and make small talk with the vignerons and wile away a good half hour complaining about the riders of the day.

Darrigade? He's solid, he's impressed many. He'll want his yellow jersey back and that boy he deserves it. Gaul? He'll never claw back the minutes he's lost. Too tired, they say, far too tired after the Giro and the effort he put in.

No, another pipes up, it's old boy Gaston Bénac – he'll find those minutes in the Pyrenees alone. Just you watch him.

The rest of the French team? Regional riders at best this year. With no one to ride for, they're showing their true colours and riding for themselves, it's just that they're not good enough. Malléjac, the boy's a doper. Mahé, he's just a big lad from Morbihan. No class. Not like Bobet.

Walkowiak – that pup? He's just keeping the yellow jersey warm for someone. OK, so he's ridden well and got himself in the right breakaways but you'd be insane if you think that chubby-cheeked regional rider is going to join the likes of Coppi, Kubler, Bartali, Bobet and Leducq himself.

Perhaps Laurédi, he's getting to the right age now. Without Louison around, he's just the sort who could make a difference.

But why, Leducq wonders, why do they have to go so quickly? They're ahead of the schedule every day, it's as if they're all trying to shake each other off. All this speed. There was a time when the Tour was attritional. You'd grind your opponents down, you'd grit your teeth and stop occasionally – always together – trying to psych out your rivals.

Why, you'd probably stop at one of these vignerons.

A top-up? Why, I don't mind if I do.

You see, Leducq wonders, they're missing out on so much. This stage – Angers to La Rochelle. The history, the ground on which so many battles were fought. Did you know, for instance, that 90km in, the riders would be crossing the Ponts-de-Cé, scene of one of France's most famous battles.

Admire the Ponts de Cé

But the peloton is not for slowing down, nor is it for admiring the Ponts de Cé or any other bridges indeed. Following the template laid down by previous stages, gunshots are fired – any number of daredevil escapees rush out of the peloton only

Why do they have to go so fast?

to be hauled back in – before a clutch of riders are allowed to ride free. All eyes are of course on the new yellow jersey, Roger Walkowiak, who has both eyes on the breakaway, and has let free the Spaniard Poblet along with a couple of others who pose no threat to the yellow jersey.

It's Darrigade, who else, who decides that the breakaway needs to be brought to heel. After yesterday's losses, he has the most to gain. A gap of over 7 minutes means the routier-sprinter has to start cutting away at the yellow jersey's lead. Walkowiak goes with him and brings along a host of hangers-on, not least the dangerous Belgian rider Adriaenssens, as well as Nencini the Italian.

Adolphe Deledda tracks his man and joins the group.

The breakaway maintains over a four-minute lead but once more, none of them poses any serious threat, but the duo of Walkowiak and Deledda is keeping watch over any attempts to cut that four-minute lead down. Darrigade is kept firmly behind Deledda's wheel for as long as the veteran can hold him there. Walkowiak is alongside Bahamontes who also has a stake in the stage: his teammate Miguel Poblet is off the front and is desperate to win a stage.

Miguel and the Hat-trick

Miguel's career has suddenly blossomed this year. He turned pro in 1944, at the tender age of 16. 12 years later, and Miguel has lost most of his hair, something that his more hirsute peloton colleagues are keen to poke fun of. It's less visible from the back, so Miguel tries as often as possible to ride from the front.

The Tour de France is the third of the grand tours, and Miguel is hunting for a very specific record – to be the first man in history to win stages in all three grand tours of the same year. He won four at the Giro, and three at the Vuelta. And all of this has come since Miguel left Spain to seek his fortune just two years ago. There's no money in Spanish cycling, you see.

His father was unusual among the fathers of the peloton – he actively encouraged his son to ride a bike. Poblet Senior owned a bike shop, and forced his son to go beyond his sprinting abilities, making him climb a steep 300m hill every single day. It was this training that helped Poblet Junior win the National Mountains Championships in Spain three times before leaving for France, and then in last year's Tour he took all mountains points at the top of the Tourmalet.

Poblet's escapade is aided ably by the Englishman Brian Robinson, who has spent the last few days trying to explain to everyone that he is not from London, that he does not drink tea and eat cake every day at 4pm and that he is, in fact, a hard-as-nails Yorkshireman. A profile in the daily sports paper has portrayed him as a tea-supping southerner, and Robinson is furious. With Poblet, he is taking it out on the road.

They are joined by Louis Caput, the Dutchmen Nolten and De Groot, the two tricolores Privat and Mahé, the Belgian Adriaenssens and Poblet's colleague Lorono. Behind, various groups are forming and un-forming in a fluid, liquid chase that is sparked principally by various riders' desire to reach the front group and take some more time back on the yellow jersey.

When that chase group does coalesce, the main participants are Walkowiak, Darrigade, Bahamontes, De Bruyne, Bover (another Spaniard), Deledda, Wagtmans and Roger Hassenforder. All have a stake, one way or another, which is partly what makes it such a fascinating chase. Darrigade is trying to ride Walkowiak off his wheel. Deledda keeps pulling him back. Bahamontes and Bover are taking turns

Why do they have to go so fast?

on the front to deliberately slow the group down, much to Darrigade's frustration. Hassenforder is trying to slow things down for Louis Caput who is in the front group. As different riders hit the front, the chase group stretches and strains, and then relaxes depending on the ambitions of the front rider.

A Darrigade group eventually breaks away and Walkowiak and Deledda have decided that he can take some time as they drop back. Not too much, but enough. Let him ride.

The Tour is taking shape, although what shape – nobody knows.

In time, this chase group agrees that the task in hand is to reduce the gap, rather than to join the front group. The blackboards inform the leaders that they have over 3 minutes on the chasers, and this allows them to slow down and start checking each other out. Jan Adriaenssens is receiving threatening glares. He won't pull from the front. Nolten has disappeared – a puncture they think – and his teammate Dan De Groot is leading the front group into La Rochelle.

It's all pretty gardens and fountains, sharp hills and sharper descents, brisk breezes and wind tunnels. La Rochelle is a pretty town to end a stage in.

Poblet and Caput detach themselves from the group as the riders enter the velodrome and De Groot gives up – it's between these two. Louis Caput, the little man from Brittany with the long career behind him, looking for more money for the Ouest team. Miguel Poblet, looking to be the first man to win stages in three grand tours in one year. The dust is kicking up behind them, and Poblet leads as they enter the home straight. Caput is in perfect position, but Poblet is strong – so strong, those legs that climbed every day of his youth are holding him in good stead, and that bald head arches over his handlebars as he takes the stage with a half a wheel's length ahead of little Louis, many years his senior but in appearance, you would think not.

Poblet keeps on riding, punching the air, taking a victory lap or two. Does anyone know about his achievement? Who cares. For Miguel, this is everything.

A few minutes later, the chase group enters, and André Darrigade takes the peloton sprint

Allez, Gégène

But on a day where many have been bemoaning the frenzy of the modern Tour, spare a thought for Eugène Letendre, the Ouest rider who rode past the vignerons at Coteaux de Layon a full two minutes later than the peloton. Letendre, that admirable colleague of Roger Hassenforder who was sharing his Calvados with the peloton just a few days ago, was struggling to keep up with those same riders just a handful of kilometres into today's stage.

"Ah Letendre," shouted Gaston Benac, wine glass in hand, saucisson sec in mouth. "Allez Gégène, Allez!"

And then, with Letendre out of earshot, Bénac turns to his dégustation friends, and mutters:

"Il est foutu, ce jeune."

He's fucked.

Others shouted their encouragements, but for Letendre, the Tour was already over. Not used to riding at such high speeds with such regularity, Letendre was one of relatively few victims of this Tour à haute vitesse. The Breton would fight throughout the day, averaging a meagre 30km per hour, before reaching the control outside the time cut-off.

By the time Eugène entered the La Rochelle velodrome, the crowds had mostly already gone. Miguel Poblet was already out on the town with his bouquet of flowers and, courtesy of Louison Bobet, a peaked cap with a feather. Bobet had recently

Why do they have to go so fast?

been awarded the status of Chevalier des fins dégustateurs, because, well, because he's Louison. His responsibility, as Chevalier, was to induct today's winner, who accepted the hat with good grace. It covers up the baldness.

For Letendre, then, the Tour is over. For Miguel, his year is complete.

Hassen-le-Magnifique
13th July 1956
Stage 9, La Rochelle to Bordeaux, 214km

Yellow, not Walkowiak

There's the yellow jersey! Look – it's the yellow jersey!

The peloton rolls out of La Rochelle and still hardly anybody knows the name of Roger Walkowiak. Or at least, hardly anyone can pronounce Walkowiak.

Still, he's just keeping the jersey warm for someone else, so there won't be any need to remember the name.

The newspapers have made clear that this is a temporary exercise:

"Walkowiak is a country-boy lost in the city. His boss Sauveur Ducazeaux is an inn-keeper in civilian's clothing. Together, the two of them are tilting at windmills. They'll think that they've come a long way, especially after the Vuelta where Walkowiak walked out on the French team halfway between signing-on and departing."

Antoine Blondin, L'Equipe

Blondin is one of France's finest sportswriters, but – thinks Ducazeaux – he's also a twat. The Nord-Est-Centre technical director is a former Tour stage winner who retired to the Basque country to run a restaurant but found himself wanted once more in the sport he loved so much. An inn-keeper in civilian's clothing, he huffs. And my boy, a country boy lost in the city, he fumes. I'll show them.

Blondin has hit a nerve, however. He's right about the Vuelta, which was one of Ducazeaux's lowest moments in cycling. And Walkowiak's, come to mention it.

While Marcel Bidot takes charge of the French team in the Tour de France, Ducazeaux takes charge for the Giro and the Vuelta. Lesser competitions, lesser management, so they might say. Ducazeaux takes them just as seriously, which is more than could be said for his team. Having won the Vuelta with Jean Dotto the year before, Ducazeaux had gone into the '56 edition with confidence. Bobet had shown signs that he would maintain his '55 form, and Walkowiak's 2nd place in the Dauphiné last year meant that he would be a valuable lieutenant.

Walkowiak had won the stage into Pampluna, but Louison Bobet's saddle sores were causing him no shortage of trouble, and the French team's morale dipped along with Bobet's form. As Bobet pulled out of the Vuelta, so did a number of his colleagues, leaving Ducazeaux furious with his riders.

On the road to Bilbao, Jean Dotto turns to Roger Walkowiak and says:

"You know what Roger, my wife's here and what are we doing? Dragging ourselves to the finish line? Louison's gone, and so am I."

Dotto knew he had got lucky last year and there was no chance of a repeat.

With Gilbert Bauvin in the top 10, Ducazeaux needed support for his team leader. But Telotte and Bergaud pulled out the next morning, claiming injuries. Dotto himself had given up, while Jean Bobet and Claude Le Ber were riding like it was a Sunday afternoon. Every man could claim some kind of injury – even Dotto had suffered a fall – except for Walkowiak.

So when Walkowiak got off his bike and walked away from the Vuelta, Ducazeaux exploded with rage.

"You have no excuse, young man. No injury. You have disappointed me. You'll never ride for me again. Ever. Don't you forget that. I'll never select you for any of my teams ever again."

So why did Roger Walkowiak give up? Perhaps because everyone else had. It seemed to be the thing to do. Bauvin was too far back in the general classification to be a serious contender, and the rest of the team had already taken the train. Ducazeaux's reaction had shocked him, though. Walkowiak sat down to write an apology, and with Raphaël Géminiani pleading his case (he can be a useful ally - if he manages your trade team), Ducazeaux quickly calmed.

Perhaps I was hasty, he thought. I'm prone to the odd outburst. He's a good boy, Roger.

I'll let him stew for a while, though. And then I'll pick him for the Nord-Est-Centre team. After all, I'm a man down without that idiot Hassenforder.

Ducazeaux throws L'Equipe out of the car window for some lucky fan to collect, and swears never to read Antoine Blondin ever again. And if Roger wins the Tour, he'll ram his article right down his throat.

A Dutch Escape

Van der Pluym, another name the locals struggle to pronounce, is rather typically the first man out of the blocks. The Dutch have made a name for themselves of getting into breakaways and trying to pull the Tour along at a high pace. They're trying to capture as much bonus money and as many places as they can before the mountains arrive so they can position Gerrit Voorting for a tilt at the big prize.

He's quickly joined though, as 17 men break out of the peloton – most notably the yellow jersey himself, and we go through the motions of what has become something of a standard during this Tour – chasers escape the peloton and attempt to close down the gap. Roger Hassenforder, who else, is leading the third charge to close down the 18-strong lead group, and between 60km and 70km, he does so, dragging along a clutch of out-of-breath hangers-on. Roger smiles. This might be his kind of day.

Next, the peloton shatters once more. Brankart, Ockers, Darrigade and Laurédi break free and bridge the gap from peloton to breakaway, but where is Charly Gaul? Once more, as has become the custom, the Luxembourg rider is idling away at the back of the peloton. Murmurs of "who does he think he is" are whispered among the journalistic community. Who indeed, does Gaul think he is? He wins the Giro and thinks he can dawdle every day losing 10 minutes on average?

Even Gaul is stirred into action, however. A few more kilometres and everyone would be together once more.

Louis Caput had already proved himself to be an excellent influence on Roger Hassenforder. After Francis Pelissier and Antonin Magne had both tried – and failed – to rein in the Alsacien's worst and most destructive instincts, Caput the teammate was turning into Caput the man-manager.

"You know what happens next..." he suggests to Hassenforder.

Roger shrugs a daft shrug.

"The peloton's back together. We're going to slow down."

A look of realisation falls upon Roger Hassenforder's face.

"Don't waste any time. Go."

Hassen-le-Magnifique

Hassen Attacks

And go he did, leaving the somnolent peloton behind, looking back to find only Trexel and Arie Van der Pluym had responded. With 100km to go, this would have to be one of Roger Hassenforder's deepest efforts. Nose into the wind, Hassenforder launches attack after attack, trying to distance the peloton even further. One minute, two minutes, up to three minutes, with Trexel and Van der Pluym gasping in his wake.

The Alsacien barely has time to acknowledge the blackboards and doesn't want to know the number of kilometres left to Bordeaux. He's head down, determined.

Hassenforder pulls up alongside Felix Levitan's car and yells:

"Oi, what about the combativity prize? You giving it to Darrigade – again?"

Levitan laughs. "You've got three minutes on them, lad."

"Merci Monsieur Levitan," beams Hassenforder. A smile that could melt the ice caps. It's hard not to forgive Hassenforder when he's at his peak. Eccentric, perhaps, and a character the Tour would be weaker without.

Trexel is suffering. Hassenforder offers him some water from his bidon and the two men acknowledge each other, silently, before the Swiss rider acknowledges his day is over and drops back towards the peloton, through the peloton itself and into anonymity, from whence he came.

Van der Pluym attacks, but Hassenforder is straight on to him. The lingua franca here is German:

"Do that once more and I'll stick to your wheel all the way to the finish and I won't give you an inch."

The Dutchman falls into line, and there's even a moment for the riders to acknowledge the vines as they pass through Blaye. Côtes de Blaye, insists Hassenforder, proferring an imaginary glass to his breakaway colleagues. Rouge. But it's better where I come from. Du blanc. Du bon. They wave at the wine stalls lining the road, the local vignerons of the day hoping to attract a Gaston Bénac or an André Leducq, perhaps a photo with somebody famous to hang in their vestibule for people who come along to taste of a Saturday afternoon. And then there's so many vignerons that it becomes boring, and they focus on their riding again.

25,000 spectators welcomed Roger Hassenforder into the velodrome for what was a formality. A solo breakaway of two men, if such a thing were possible, and one of Roger Hassenforder's finest moments. Van der Pluym finds it almost rude to compete against him, but he tries, for show.

In all this, the Tour has passed through the vineyards of Bordeaux, it has run parallel to the Atlantic with its sumptuous greens and its majestic greys, it has gone through Royan, within sight of the old Cordouan lighthouse in the estuary, the beach and the sunshine poking through grey clouds amongst blue skies and yet no one speaks of any sight other than that of Roger Hassenforder, Hassen-le-Magnifique.

The peloton has pulled back to within one minute of the valiant winner, and that peloton includes the mild-mannered Roger Walkowiak, still in yellow, still in disbelief, and welcomed by his wife Pierrette, into whose arms he falls, tears falling down his face.

"You made it, Roger, you made it."

"I did. And have you seen my jersey? I wore it for you."

Sauveur Ducazeaux looks on at the happy couple and thinks to himself: "Ahhh young love. Well, I've held my part of the bargain. Despite my better instincts. Now you need to lose that jersey, boy."

Hassen-le-Magnifique

Bobet and Gem

Louison Bobet is on his haunches, knees either side of Raphaël Géminiani's head, which is lying – with the rest of his prostrate body – on the inner field of the Bordeaux velodrome. The crowds have departed. The Walkowiaks have departed, arm in arm. A day of rest lies ahead, but for Raphaël Géminiani, a week of rest would be insufficient.

Géminiani has had a bad year. His time is not yet up, but his body is crying out for rest, for less hard work. This is a man who should have won a Tour already, if not two. So close to greatness, and yet so far. 1951 could have been his year, but Hugo Koblet was climbing trees without breaking a sweat. That feels an era ago right now, after an era spent protecting his friend Louison.

"They're killing us, Louison. Killing us," he cries.

Bobet pulls himself to the ground. A month without riding the bike has left him creaky and uncertain of his own body. The saddle sores don't help either.

"You're not yourself, are you?"

"I am myself. I'm very much myself, Louison. But I've just ridden 9 classics in 9 days. 9 classics! You think you can ride a Tour like this? You'd have to do it without me."

Bobet sits and sighs. This is a Tour that he could have controlled, by force of personality. There would be no fighting in the French team. Géminiani would have been put to use. Bauvin would have been a régionale, where he belongs. Hassenforder would never have been given such a long leash.

Instead, it's chaos. Nobody is working for anybody, it's every man for himself. He looks at his best friend Top Gun, le Grand Fusil stretched out on the grass and thinks, what have they done to him? What are they doing to each other?

Enter (and exit) Pierrette Walkowiak
14th July 1956
Rest day, Bordeaux

Lose The Wife

Sauveur Ducazeaux looked upon the happy couple yesterday as they embraced in the velodrome and he will concede that a tear came to his eye. He had allowed his young charge to keep the yellow jersey until this moment and next came his part of the bargain – lose it.

Lose the yellow jersey, and you lose the target on your back. Let someone else suffer the constant attacks, maybe a Belgian or a Dutchman. We don't have the team to defend this yellow jersey, so it doesn't matter how much you enjoy wearing it and how much your wife admires you in it, you have to lose it.

But first – lose the wife.

Pierrette and Roger had met at a ball organised after the Grand Prix de Commentry two years ago, close to their home town of Montluçon. Pierrette was a secretary at the Miner's Welfare Society in Montluçon, Roger a former metalworker turned professional cyclist. Turned water-carrier.

Earlier in the day, Roger had participated in the traditional Grand Prix, hoping to win in front of his friends and family. No such luck. A puncture, a minor fall, and a chase to get back to the front group left Roger sweaty, tired and cursing his bad luck. Well, he thought, my day can't get any worse.

Roger the wallflower supped at his drink, desperately holding conversations with friends so that he didn't have to dance. An introduction followed a further introduction, and by multiple degrees of friendship, Roger was introduced to a girl someone knows called Pierrette.

Slender-faced, gracious and intensely pretty, Pierrette Lajarge made effortless small talk. Yes, I noticed you in the race earlier (she did not), ah I think I saw you in the crowd earlier (he did not), would you care to dance (he cannot), perhaps you'd be able to meet me again, maybe at the ball in Montluçon itself in two weeks' time, organised by my club, but only if you're able (she is).

This time, Roger made sure to wash, comb his hair, wear his finest suit. They agreed to meet again, this time sooner, and then more frequently. Mme Walkowiak was introduced to Mlle Lajarge, Mme Walkowiak approved, although she could do with a little fattening up, those aren't child-bearing hips, a girl could do with some weight around her, Roger.

It is not a coincidence that Roger's bounce in form came shortly after meeting Pierrette; Roger had not been living the life of a dedicated sportsman. Living at home with his mother, Roger ate whatever his mother prepared for him. If it's lard, it's lard, and plenty of it. If it's andouillette, it's andouillette. And so on. Old Mother Walkowiak had no time for the sporting life and its demands upon her kitchen. It was her kitchen, after all. Boy, you will eat and you will eat until you burst, because God alone knows when there may not be food on this table again.

Pierrette understood the needs of the professional cyclist, and took part in the transformation of Roger Walkowiak from also-ran to yellow jersey and – in the eyes of Sauveur

Enter (and exit) Pierrette Walkowiak

Ducazeaux at least – potential Tour de France winner. Pierrette took charge the day they moved in together, and everything from sleep to exercise and diet was carefully managed and based around Roger's racing calendar.

The happy couple moved quickly and married over Christmas of 1955; the young Walkowiak's sporting career had already taken an upward curve with a brave performance in the Dauphiné that year. The new, slimmer Roger Walkowiak had matched Louison Bobet in the mountains for every pedal stroke. Bobet shook his hand, commented that few men had pushed him this hard. Nobody else noticed, but Pierrette did.

And so, knowing the importance of Pierrette in Roger Walkowiak's life, and indeed the affection he holds for her, it is a wrench for Sauveur Ducazeaux. He admires Pierrette, principally for her culinary skills.

Nonetheless, the wife has to go.

Interrupting the two lovers, Ducazeaux is himself interrupted.

"Monsieur," interjects the wife, silencing Ducazeaux before he can speak, pressing two palms to his chest.

"I've come by car with friends. They're leaving this evening and quite naturally they suggested I go with them. But I think I'll stay twenty-four hours and leave tomorrow evening."

Ducazeaux looks across at the disturbingly approving face of his yellow jersey. He looks back at Pierrette and inhales. This is going to be hard.

"Out of the question. You've seen your husband, and you've embraced him. You will have noticed that he's in good health. I know that you've communicated to him your confidence and your faith in his abilities. But that's enough. Your job here is done. Now you have to leave."

Calm, but firm. That's the way to deal with it, he reassures himself. The lovers' faces have fallen.

"Oh come, come. Don't wallow in melancholy. Compare this small sacrifice I'm asking of you with the greater satisfaction that awaits you. You don't win the Tour de France on your honeymoon now, do you?"

Four cow-eyes are still pleading with him.

"Madame, you have to leave."

Ducazeaux himself accompanies Pierrette out of the hotel, offering assurances as they walk.

"But Mr Ducazeaux, Roger and I…"

"Yes, yes, I know. We have, on the one hand, what I understand… and on the other, we have the Tour. A rider who is trying to win the Tour should only think of victory. I know you're a reasonable woman, but that is not enough. Your presence alone is enough to soften my rider. He shouldn't feel like he's on holiday when I want him to feel like he's going into battle."

Ducazeaux sat down later that evening to write in his diary. He wrote:

"Now is the time to reflect on a job well done, so far. The rest day must not break the rhythm we have created. Tomorrow, I'll make them ride. I'll be with them. We'll talk. I'll remind Roger of his promise to return to the ranks. Mario Bertolo and Pierre Scribante will help Roger in the Pyrenees, and I'll keep Adolphe Deledda for the end. If everything goes as I have planned, we'll need him."

He then walked down to the kitchens and ordered the chefs out. Dégagez-vous, non j'ai pas besoin d'aide, allez.

There was work to do.

From now on, fini the drinks at the back of the peloton. Fini the second helpings at the dinner table. Fini the champagne, at least until Paris.

Leave the drinking to the Bretons.

Operation "Lose the Yellow Jersey"
15th July 1956
Stage 10, Bordeaux to Bayonne, 201km

Hard Men In The Rain

201km to cover, and the weather has turned. Bordeaux is wet, and every rider bar one is wearing their transparent rain jackets. That rider is the Breton tricolore Francois Mahé. The man from Morbihan isn't even wearing a cap, because – obviously – they make them tough in Brittany. Mahé, as if to prove the point, is the first to make the attempt to break away from the peloton, a peloton in which Roger Walkowiak is studiously integrating himself alongside the men he fears most in the mountains, Ockers and Brankart.

Gaul, naturally, tags along at the back. Charly Gaul has now lost nearly an hour on the front men. Is there really any point in him continuing?

Today is the last flat stage before the mountains. Tomorrow is one of the most feared stages of the Tour, Bayonne to Pau, followed the next day by Pau-Luchon. Those mountains are visible in the distance, as if to remind the sprinters that they have one more day to themselves before they have to focus on getting back before the cut-off time. Every day.

Up front, 9 men have made the first move, and they include André Darrigade and Fred Debruyne, the two men most likely to make the sprint finish, if indeed it comes to that. Those 9 men are quickly joined by others who find the pace of the peloton a little pedestrian, and the press favourite Nello Laurédi has found himself carried along with Dutch fan favourite Gerrit Voorting and Belgian rouleur Jan Adriaenssens.

And for a moment, as the rain stops and the sun pokes out from between the clouds, the breakaway of what is eventually 19 men starts to slow, while the peloton behind appears to be catching. This is perhaps all going too quickly for Roger Walkowiak whose mission today is to end up wearing the rather fetching violet jersey of the Nord-Est-Centre team while someone else carries the burden of yellow for a week or so. Don't lose too much time, stay with the climbers.

Ah yes, but which ones, you might wonder? Brankart and Ockers, perhaps. Gaul? No, he's not even bothered this year. Deledda reminds him to keep an eye on the blackboards and he's employed Huyghes and Scodeller to relay between the group and the team cars. They're putting the new radios to use, and Sauveur Ducazeaux is having it explained to him regularly by younger people. Press this button to speak, Sauveur. No, this button. And then speak. Oh, I'll do it…

And almost by coincidence, the peloton slows to a crawl. This infuriates the Ouest rider Louis Caput who berates his colleagues for not putting in the effort but he is met by shrugs and a general non-committal grunt from members of other teams who simply don't fancy chasing down their colleagues in the breakaway with any vim or vigour.

Bienvenue chez les Darrigade

At the front, the leaders are venturing further south and deeper into the Landes, home of André Darrigade. A foray into Dax, his home town, would usually be the opportunity to stop, hug friends and family, pose for a photograph with some local dignitary, maybe even have a drink, but not today. André Darrigade still scents yellow, as well he might, but he does ask his breakaway colleagues if he can lead them through Dax and at a few kilometres per hour less than usual, to which they give their assent, and the blond routier-sprinter takes them into his home town.

An enormous banner is visible to all, and perhaps even to all from the next town. It proclaims:

"Bravo! Darrigade", and just below that, denoting the hierarchy of affections for local Daxois riders, a simple "Allez Dolhats!" in a somewhat smaller choice of letters, perhaps a little hurried. An afterthought. But a nice one nonetheless for the other rider from Dax, Albert Dolhats, who simply isn't quite as good as the other one. The good one. The fast one.

As the journalists wind through behind the breakaway, they take a minute to admire the crowds, the noise, the fervour. They've come out for Darrigade here. There's a band. Music playing. Fans hanging from windows, on rooftops. It's a shame he couldn't have been in yellow, murmurs Chassaignon. That would have made it truly special.

Bénac has his mouth around a local sausage, given free of charge by a roadside vendor, but he mutters his agreement, scattering baguette crumbs as he does so.

Two cars next year, thinks Chassaignon. That's all I ask.

The yellow jersey gets a rapturous reception when he does pass through, roughly 15 minutes later, although not many could admit to being able to pronounce his name or in some cases, even knowing who he is. It's the yellow jersey. That's all, and he won't be wearing it for long.

The real riders will take over soon.

No Fairytale in Bayonne

Bayonne arrives along with another storm, and the local boy enters the velodrome in 6th position. Debruyne has manoeuvred himself brilliantly with his teammates in support, and who does Darrigade have? Forestier, Bauvin and Mahé, all behind him and none of them particularly supportive.

So as Darrigade lashes furiously at the pedals, Debruyne is given the perfect flying sprint to the finish, and he takes another stage with absolute ease, while a general groan falls upon the velodrome as they learn that André Darrigade has not won the stage, and most likely will not end up in yellow this evening.

No fairytale in Bayonne.

As it happens, it's Geerit Voorting who appears to be in yellow, with Nello Laurédi not far behind. These two have been hanging around the top positions for the last week without having come to prominence, but the Dutchman in yellow and the Franco-Italian in 3rd would now look towards the mountains where they are expected to ride well, while Darrigade in 2nd would have to convince everyone that he's not just a sprinter-routier, he's an all-rounder.

And Walkowiak? He finishes the day 9 minutes back behind Voorting. And he knows that the consensus will be that he has gone back to where he belongs. He was never going to carry the yellow jersey into the Pyrenees, he was never good enough, leave it to the big boys now, Roger Walkowhatsyourname.

Adolphe Deledda understands what's going through his team leader's mind as he watches Geerit Voorting pull on the prized jersey.

"You're worried about what everyone else thinks, aren't you?" he asks him, rhetorically.

"You make me laugh. It's not losing that jersey that worries

Operation "Lose the Yellow Jersey"

you, but it's what your wife thinks, what your mother thinks, what your father and your friends think. You're afraid they think you're cooked. That's your pride talking. Think about it Roger, think about what you've just done – it's the perfect result for you. Now, instead of being the hunted, you're the hunter. You're in precisely the right place. And if they think you're no good, forget them. The Tour is like a war – you can't always be on the front line. From time to time, you have to rest. Let Voorting and the rest take the blows for us. We'll mark them and Sauveur will work it out."

So, Charly Gaul, Do You Have It?
16th July 1956
Stage 11, Bayonne to Pau, 255km

Ducazeaux's Kitchen

Sauveur Ducazeaux is no stranger to the kitchen, owning a restaurant that keeps him busy during the winter months and, he'll be the first to admit he hasn't exactly held back from partaking in good meals since he retired from his professional cycling career. A couple of stage wins earned him enough notoriety to open his restaurant and fill it with locals keen to rub shoulders with a cycling celebrity, at least until Sauveur-le-cycliste became Sauveur-le-restaurateur, by which time Sauveur was missing cycling, and cycling was missing him.

He woke at 5am this morning to chase out the head chef at the Hotel de la Gare in Bayonne, so that he could prepare the bidons and the food for his team.

With the form shown by Walkowiak, a change had come over Ducazeaux. His approach to being regional team manager had been to let the riders pretty much eat whatever they liked, so long as they stayed within the portion guidelines laid out at the start of the Tour. They could also drink during the race, but not any more. The possibility of a Tour winner meant that a new regime had to be imposed upon the team and every man had to be at peak condition to support Ducazeaux's ambition.

In the evenings, grilled meat, salads and the occasional fistful of pasta. During the race, rice and orange juice (mixed together in a bidon), and single mouthful sandwiches made with pain d'epices and honey. Enough to get you through the stage, and no more than that.

With these supplies, words of advice: "Drink as little as possible. You'll feel thirsty, but resist as much as you can the desire to drink. Wet your lips, no more than that. You see those riders falling back down the first mountainside? They'll be the ones who've been drinking. Stick to what's in your bidons and you'll cope."

A little more strategically, Ducazeaux has told Walkowiak to keep as close to the two Belgians Ockers and Brankart as he can. See how he feels on the first climb of the day, the Soulor, before taking on the Aubisque which is 500m above the peak of the Soulor. Ducazeaux has supreme confidence in his man. Writing to his wife before the stage, he expresses his absolute belief that Roger is going to win the race, and that everything is going to plan.

Is Ducazeaux deluded? The press, after all, are clamouring for a Nello Laurédi win or a Charly Gaul comeback.

The Climbers Come Back

In fact, despite Ducazeaux's insouciance, it's the latter that the riders fear most. Having seen or read about Charly's exploits in the Giro, and knowing that the young Luxembourg rider has time to make up on them all, the plan is to put nails in Gaul's coffin before he even reaches the mountains.

Bahamontes, the Eagle of Toledo, is one of the first to break away early in the stage to Pau, alongside Barbotin the tricolore, Defilippis the Italian, Van Genechten from Belgium and Le Ber the over-sized Breton. With the Spaniard leading the assault on Gaul, the five men create a 25-second gap.

Together, they are an elite hit squad, a band of brothers aligned against the dangerous Gaul. Eliminate him, before he becomes a danger to us all. They are strangers to each other. Bahamontes is a man who goes it alone. He doesn't do breakaways. Le Ber doesn't mind an escape from the peloton, but it's usually with other regionals. He knows Barbotin, but not the Italian lad. Van Genechten is here to give Ockers a chance. He doesn't care who's with him.

Their escapade doesn't last long. As the roads tighten and the overhanging trees hide chasing packs from view, the slim, slight figure of Gaul appears as if from nowhere.

"Bastards," he mutters as he slots onto their wheels, and almost as one, the band of brothers disbands. Hands are placed on top of handlebars, Le Ber sits up and Van Genechten shrugs. They made me do it. Gaul whispers something about having worked in an abattoir, and Le Ber promises not to do it again.

It won't be long before the peloton catches up and everyone is back together, so backs are slapped and Gaul is ignored and the men admire the scenery. For once, no wide roads or cobblestones, no poplar-lined avenues promising the warmth of the south, but instead the smell of burning rubber, cut hay, warm oil and the delicate scent of acacia, an assault on the senses.

The roads have narrowed, and then through valleys they widen as they run alongside babbling rivers and streams, and the road narrows again as it takes the first true ascent of this 1956 Tour de France, the Soulor. A group detaches itself from the peloton, and it includes the usual climbing suspects: Bahamontes, Gaul, Brankart, Ockers, and… Walkowiak.

It also includes Andre Darrigade, as well as Defilippis, one of the day's early Gaul-stabbers, and Adriaensens, the Belgian climber who has been climbing the general classification quietly and effectively. For Darrigade, it's an opportunity to demonstrate to Marcel Bidot that he is the man to support for the yellow jersey. There is talk of Gilbert Bauvin taking that role, but Andre has to prove himself to Bidot first. The Soulor is his first opportunity.

The climb of the Soulor lulls the non-climbers into a false sense of security. It's hard, they think, but as it levels out, lesser men believe they've conquered it. A false flat leads to a few skirmishes, but Bahamontes and Ockers take charge when the gradient accentuates. 9% and then 15% for a short while before settling at a still lung-busting 8%. A thick fog has descended as the Spaniard leaps out of his saddle and away from Ockers.

The world champion Ockers looks to his side and looks Charly Gaul straight in the eyes. Then ahead at Bahamontes. Then back at Gaul. Do you have it?

So, Charly Gaul, Do You Have It?

And then it dawns on him. He doesn't have it. Charly Gaul has nothing in the tank. He tests him, three hard pushes and he distances Gaul who has no response. Gaul's humiliation is only just beginning. Meyzenq, lanterne rouge and a pale, sick-looking youngster, is next to follow. Raymond Meyzenq, of all people, the last man in the Tour, distancing Charly Gaul, hero of the Giro. Then Valentin Huot, a climber from the less-than-successful South-West team, is another to put the sword to Charly Gaul.

Behind, a group has formed with Adriaensens, Darrigade, Brankart and Walkowiak, among others. They're just 42

So, Charly Gaul, Do You Have It?

seconds behind on the Aubisque, which like the Soulor, has seen the clouds descend upon it.

A few years back, Wim Van Est came off around here. There's a few nervous looks in the Dutch team, and a couple of riders point down the ravine. Don't look, they say. If you look, you'll end up down there.

From the safety of the team car, Sauveur Ducazeaux monitors his man, carefully scrutinising every facial gesture, every movement. He's climbing well, he thinks. He's not going into the red and yet he's just 42 seconds behind the leaders.

My boy's doing everything I'd asked of him.

It's Valentin Huot who emerges from the clouds to reach the peak of the Aubisque. The crowds know to recognise Gaul and Ockers – but Huot? Who is this? Fans five deep line the mountainside as they cheer past Huot, Bahamontes, Ockers, some young lad they've never seen before – who is this guy – check his number. Papers are rustled – Meyzenq, someone cries. Raymond Meyzenq, the lanterne rouge! Allez Raymond, the cry goes up, all too late. Some try to run after him, encourage him, Allez Raymond!

But where's Charly Gaul?

They all came out to see Charly Gaul. The papers promised Charly Gaul. They'd have 40 seconds to wait, and quietly, ever so quietly, a man in violet rides past them, his cheeks puffed out, as always, but a picture of calm. We're into the regional riders, someone would say, not knowing this was the man who held yellow just a few days ago.

On the descent of the Aubisque, the lead group is caught without necessarily making too much effort not to be caught. Together, they make a cosmopolitan, multi-talented peloton, one that includes André Darrigade and Charly Gaul, Federico Bahamontes and Roger Walkowiak. Raymond Meyzenq and Valentin Huot.

WALKO

A Tentative Agreement

There's a tentative agreement that the sprinters should be left to compete for the prize and for André Darrigade, there's the possibility – calculations permitting – that the yellow jersey is returning to his broad shoulders. Who would have thought that this sprinter-routier would have tackled the double climbs of the Soulor and the Aubisque, and then descend the mountain to wrest the yellow jersey from the absent Dutchman Voorting?

Alas, no stage win for Darrigade – the Italian Defilippis has the edge on him today, but Marcel Bidot is beaming as his sprinter makes it home in third.

"You're in yellow, André! You've done it again, my boy."

"I told you I could climb, Marcel. I told you, didn't I?"

They embrace, and Bidot's job is made a little easier for him. Perhaps Darrigade could take the yellow jersey all the way across the Alps and all the way to Paris. The boy's done the Aubisque and has descended like a demon all the way in to Pau. Over his shoulder, he sees Nello Laurédi, he sees Jan Adriaenssens, he sees his own teammate Gilbert Bauvin. Instead of seeing those who might wear yellow tomorrow, he sees those who might steal yellow from him tomorrow.

For André, everything is possible.

Jempy Schmitz's Awesome Adventure
17th July 1956
Stage 12, Pau to Luchon, 130km

Dangermen from the Duchy

Luxembourg's team manager Nicolas Frantz has quite the opposite problem to his French counterpart Bidot. In Charly Gaul, he had one of the favourites of the Tour, and in his Luxembourg team he had a band of mercenaries willing to give their all for the shared proceeds that would doubtless come from a Gaul victory. Or at least, that is what they were assured when they signed up. Of course, putting together a team for Luxembourg is the devil's own job, and there are quality riders without a team, if you look hard enough.

The Portuguese rider Barbosa had been seduced by Gaul's Giro victory. A Tour slogging on his behalf would make him rich, if Gaul could reproduce such form. Brian Robinson was just glad of the ride, the British team having been disbanded since last year's derring-do adventures, and for Robinson, a glittering future would surely await as the manufacturer team managers take note of his own performances, Gaul or no Gaul.

The problem for Frantz is that there really is no Gaul. Of course, he's there in person, but the Gaul we all knew from the Giro is no longer with us. The Gaul that has come to the Tour has spent the first 9 stages of this race languishing ten minutes behind the peloton, accumulating losses that in a casino would have seen him bankrupt. He had played all his cards running up over an hour's deficit on the leader, and when Stan Ockers read his face on the col de Soulor yesterday, word got round quickly that Gaul was a busted flush.

And so the band of domestiques were set free, starting with the Portuguese Barbosa, part of the initial breakaway that had eight minutes over the peloton at Sainte-Marie-du-Campan. It was around this point that his teammate – and native Luxemburger – Jean-Pierre (Jempy) Schmitz decided he would bridge the 8-minute gap. He would have seen the blackboards, so what made Jempy Schmitz take up the challenge? Perhaps he was feeling good, perhaps he just thought to himself – why not? What do I have to lose?

By the time Barbosa and company had reached the foot of the Aspin, Jempy Schmitz had bridged that gap. An effort so deep that you would have forgiven him for taking it easy up the Aspin. Not today.

With Barbosa and Schmitz taking the leaders with them at the foot of the Aspin, you may have been forgiven for thinking that this was 'classic race tactics'. The very idea of putting two teammates in the breakaway ahead of two of the biggest climbs of the Tour, the Aspin and the Peyresourde, is good old-fashioned Tour thinking. There were some grumblings in the peloton once word got around that two of Gaul's teammates were in the breakaway and that they were digging deep to widen the gap between themselves and the rest of the riders.

Mark Gaul, they said, he's up to something. He's got the legs today, just watch him bridge that gap.

But Gaul didn't have the legs. This wasn't "classic Tour

strategy", and this wasn't classic Gaul. This was exactly what Nicolas Frantz had realised yesterday and exactly what he'd told his team. If you can get in the breakaway today, do it. If you feel good, go hard and go deep. And then, if you've got a big enough gap on the peloton, enjoy yourself.

That's all there is left to do.

Well, there's that and the St. Raphael Trophy for the Grand Prix de la Montagne. Valentin Huot leads that one, for now. There are points available if you'd like them.

Jempy Schmitz wanted them more than his Portuguese teammate as he followed De Fillippis over the top of the Aspin, Barbosa lagging behind. The two worked in tandem on the descent before the Italian's back wheel juddered and slid out of line with the front wheel. De Filippis, in an instant, was off the road – safe, thank heavens – but out of the running. Jempy looks his teammate Barbosa in the eyes.

You coming? Because I'm going for it.

Barbosa shakes his head. You go. Do it.

And out of his saddle, Jempy Schmitz enters the valley and breathes the clear air, several lungs full, and thinks to himself – I still feel good. How do I still feel so good?

French Fractures

Further back down the road, while Schmitz was dancing up the Peyresourde, the man in yellow was finding the day somewhat less easy. Having already dropped behind his teammates on the first hairpins of the Aspin, it took Barbotin and Geminiani to pull André Darrigade up almost by his hair. I dug too deep yesterday, he moaned, I'll be alright if I get over the Aspin. I'll be fine. Drag me to the top, I'll catch them on the way down, just you watch. Just you watch.

And drag him they did, descending as the French expression

would have it, 'à tombeau ouverte'. In between the feeding station and the foot of the Peyresourde, Barbotin and Géminiani had selflessly reintegrated the yellow jersey back into the peloton and it was smiles all round. André, dear boy. Don't go missing again.

Gilbert Bauvin glanced back over his shoulder. Shit. He's back.

If fractures were beginning to appear in this French team, it was Gilbert Bauvin's ambition that had caused the first fissure. Bauvin could climb. By reputation, he could climb far better than Darrigade and if André couldn't keep up with him over the Peyresourde, he'd be the top French rider. Or at least, the top French Team rider. There's always Laurédi, for as long as he carries on.

Annoyingly, Bauvin was right. Darrigade's personal struggles continued on the Peyresourde. The tandem of Barbotin and Géminiani pulled back from the assembled tricolores to sit in front of the yellow jersey giving him a slipstream to ride into. Marcel Bidot, leaning out of the team car, took turns in encouraging Darrigade and then moving ahead to encourage Bauvin.

Fractures.

Darrigade sat on and watched the backs of his rivals. Walkowiak, Adriaensens and Laurédi had all been and gone. Ockers and the other kings of the mountains too. He could feel yellow being ripped from his shoulders, and the peak of the Peyresourde couldn't come soon enough. Limit the losses, shouts Geminiani. Don't give up, shouts Barbotin. The worst that can happen is you lose a handful of minutes.

A handful quickly turned into 15 as Darrigade's personal torment continued, slowly.

40 Degrees In The Shade

Further up, Jean-Pierre Schmitz's day was improving with every pedal stroke. Jempy Schmitz loved the hot weather, and he was getting plenty of it today. 40 degrees in the shade – at least further down the mountain – and the Luxembourg rider was soloing to victory, his breakaway colleagues unable to maintain the pace of the Peyresourde.

This isn't a mountain that inspires fear in men, although it ought to. The rolling greens lull a rider into a false sense of security. Gusts of wind and burning sunshine in the open can punish the unaware. Never does the Peyresourde offer actual respite. While you're admiring the rolling green moss and the landscape ahead of you, the gradients have randomised themselves, turning from 5% to 15% and back down to 3% before ramping up again. There is no consistency to the Peyresourde, contrary to appearances.

The closer Jempy Schmitz gets to the top and the hairpin bends, the more the effort starts to tell. The descent is a welcome relief.

And now, as the flamme rouge approaches, Jempy Schmitz arches his camel back and digs in, the descent down the Peyresourde having recharged his batteries sufficiently that he's able to find the legs for a sprint, not that a sprint is required, but Jempy Schmitz hasn't yet worked out that he's going to win. He's been studiously ignoring the blackboards which consistently give him over two minutes ahead of the chasers, he's been studiously ignoring the lines of girls in skimpy summer dresses, their low-cut tops, their unfashionably high hem-lines, their coquettish smiles. He's tried as hard as possible to ignore the crowds five-deep, running alongside him, moving out of the way at the last second. He's been in a world of his own, racing ahead of imaginary figures far closer than Picot, Ruiz, Morvan, Van Genechten and Huot actually are.

Schmitz has pulled off one of the most incredible Tour victories of all time, not just in his career, but in any career. From 8 minutes back just 50km into the stage, he rallied to the foot of the first climb and was a match for everyone but the Italian De Filippis. When his opportunity came on the descent of the Aspin, he took it with both hands and increased his lead on the way up the Peyresourde. The flamme rouge is the first moment Jempy Schmitz, this discreet, quiet and honourable 24-year-old, realises that he's going to win a stage.

He looks up, finally, and takes it in. Luchon, this mythical stage finish town, lies at his feet. He holds his hands to his face in disbelief, crosses the line and falls into the arms of anyone who will hold him.

A little over 6 minutes later, his team leader Charly Gaul crosses the line, arms splayed over the top of his handlebars, relief etched across his face as another day is crossed off this awful Tour. But when he realises that Jean-Pierre has won the stage, his eyes light up and a huge, beaming smile cuts across his face.

"You little beauty," he exclaims, wrapping his arms around Jempy's shoulders.

It would be a further 9 minutes before the appearance of André Darrigade, a 9-minute wait during which Jan Adriaenssens, the young Belgian rouleur, realised that he would be wearing yellow tonight. If his hopes had increased exponentially thanks to the misfiring Darrigade, then think of Laurédi, Bauvin and Walkowiak, three men whose positions in the general classification had bounced upwards and whose gaps had reduced significantly. This Tour of surprises has given us a multitude of unfashionable, unfavoured riders each with claims, and each with opportunities in the coming days.

Not least Gilbert Bauvin…

Treason Among the Tricolores
18th July 1956
Stage 13, Luchon to Toulouse, 176km

Gilbert Bauvin, (Place Money Only)

Gilbert Bauvin. Were it not for Louison Bobet's withdrawal and Jacques Anquetil's decision not to ride the Tour, would Gilbert Bauvin have been in the French team at all? Probably not. He'd have been riding for the Nord-Est-Centre team, and Roger Walkowiak would have been his loyal servant as usual, but would Gilbert Bauvin have been so prominent in the General Classification with that team around him?

Well, if Ducazeaux can get Walkowiak up there, he could certainly get Bauvin up there. Gilbert is torn.

And yet, here he is, at the start of the 13th stage with André Darrigade a handful of minutes behind and tricolore team boss Marcel Bidot avoiding making any kind of decision about whose position to defend. For Bauvin, it's obvious. If any tricolore is going to Paris in yellow then it's him, and not Monsieur le routier-sprinter. He's cooked. Burnt out. Clearly not a climber. And with one more Pyrenean stage and the Alps ahead of them, Darrigade is going backwards. Bauvin is going forwards.

Bauvin's background is typically arduous. His father was a

paver, and Gilbert was all set to follow in his father's footsteps, doing his own Tour de France des artisans, touring the country learning his trade and bringing the trade to the doorsteps of the regions. That's how it always used to be, and for many, how it always would be. The war put paid to his paving ambitions – after all, who needs a paver when the country's at war – and Gilbert ended up working as a mechanic, repairing vehicles in his native Lorraine throughout the fighting, discovering the bike later than most professional cyclists.

He came out of the war extremely poor – like most people, only more so. Riding his grandfather's ramshackle old bike, Gilbert discovered that he could ride for long periods, and climb some serious hills of which there were many around the town of Luneville. He spent his few spare centimes on new parts and inner tubes, and soon joined the local cycling club, discovering that he was a gritty, punchy little rider who was not short of a turn of speed. In his first race, he finished second despite a number of accidents, falls, thrills and spills.

"I always have problems when I'm riding well," he would later complain, and a grey cloud of bad luck would follow him throughout his career.

He often finishes second, in fact. He was second on his debut race and second in the 1953 World Cyclocross Championships, as well as 2nd in the French Cyclocross National Championships. Like a horse that prefers to follow another to the frustration of punters, Bauvin wasn't always a safe bet for victory. Place money only.

If you are a team director, Gilbert saddles you with a number of problems:

- He's kind of unlucky. He'll tell you that, and it will annoy you. But he's right.
- He speaks his mind. This would usually be OK, but

Gilbert's opinion is that he's hard done to, and it's often your fault.

- He's hard to integrate into a team. Others usually don't like him. You imagine that even Gilbert struggles to like Gilbert.
- Géminiani wouldn't ride for him. Gem would ride for Bobet, or Coppi when he rode in Italy. But he'd never ride for a "regional little whiner" like Bauvin.
- However, you might end up liking him. He's determined, he's gritty, and he never ever gives up.

And yet, here he is, 12 stages gone and this short, balding little puncheur may look like a cheap door-to-door encyclopaedia salesman, but he is the best-positioned tricolore in a sea of over-ambitious riders riding for themselves.

What is Marcel Bidot to do? Stick with the glitz and glamour of André Darrigade in the hope that yesterday was an aberration and today will be an improvement? Or does he put all his eggs in the Bauvin basket and hope that this last-minute regional replacement can fulfil his promise?

"I'm a team man," he would proclaim. "But I'm not a minion."

Year after year, Bauvin would enter the Tour de France under the Nord-Est-Centre banner, hunting for stage wins while Coppi, Kübler, Koblet, Bobet and the other superstars of the era would fight for the overall. And now, here he is.

Bauvin, Tour winner?

Once more, the press are pressing the claims of Nello Laurédi, a sort of Bauvin-lite regional rider with a more glamorous name. He's made it through two stages of the Pyrenees, slipping into the right groups without being noticed. Laurédi's advantage? Taller, slimmer, more elegant, more the 'type' of rider you'd expect to be winning the Tour.

And all of this underestimates vastly the potential of Gilbert Bauvin, a man who deserves a break. Unlike Walkowiak, he has always been ambitious. He has always aimed high, and his refusal to accept second place in an era of riders far superior to him is commendable. He will never have a better opportunity. And perhaps Marcel Bidot has this in mind as the riders prepare to leave Luchon, with two leaders in his team: the new one, Gilbert Bauvin, and the old one who still harbours hopes – André Darrigade.

For André Darrigade, there is an extra incentive today. Françoise, the new love of his life, will be waiting at the Toulouse velodrome, bouquet of flowers in her arms. He saw Pierrette waiting for Roger Walkowiak and sent a message straight away for Françoise to welcome him home. André was immune to the murmurs around the peloton that Françoise was a little – and this is putting it delicately – 'fresh' for him. They met for the first time last year. Darrigade, competing in a local criterium, Françoise, a 16-year-old girl brought by her parents. Little did they know that the blonde cyclist would be holding a candle for their little girl.

So for Marcel Bidot, two men with ambition, and just one team.

Belgium In Charge

In opposition, a Belgian team that was growing stronger by the day. They held the yellow jersey in Adriaenssens, a doughty, reliable climber, not your average sort of Belgian you'd expect to be winning Classics races every spring, but a Belgian in yellow nonetheless. And early on, Bidot would have noticed the manner in which Constantine (or Stan) Ockers was marshalling the early breakaways.

Brian Robinson, who had seen his Luxembourg teammates enjoy themselves on the breakaway yesterday, thought that in the absence of Charly Gaul's form, he'd have a go as well. Ockers didn't so much as reel him in as admonish a severe reprimand, and the Yorkshireman meekly retired to the warmth of the peloton.

Others tried, and once more it was Stan Ockers, rainbow jersey and all, springing from the bunch to remind them that Belgium was in charge today, and there would be no breakaway of any kind, not at least until the col d'Ares. Even Roger Hassenforder got a telling off – and accepted it. These are strange days indeed.

And so a relative calm falls upon the race as the riders roll through the misty fog of the valley, into the morning freshness between the flowers and the rocks, the smell of cut hay once more making certain riders sneeze, others stare misty-eyed at their childhoods passing by. La Pique flows alongside them, crashing off rocks.

It all seems so easy.

Punctures and Fractures

Perhaps the first sign that today wasn't going Marcel Bidot's way was the puncture on the Portet d'Aspet. Not a rider this time, but the Peugeot 203 – rear driver-side tyre. Ten minutes were wasted fitting the spare, so Bidot sent their other car ahead, the 4CV, to support Antonin Rolland who had also suffered a puncture. Bergaud is the next to puncture so the 4CV will have to deal with him too.

Next to go was Bauvin himself, a faller on the col de Latrape. Malléjac and Géminiani wait for him, dust him off, put him back on his bike and drag him back towards the peloton but Bauvin is losing time, and Bidot's strategy of two leaders appears less wise by the minute. In the meantime, in the front group, Darrigade has gone off with Forestier and Privat, and for Bidot this could be a double whammy – not just Darrigade back in the yellow jersey, but the Team Classification – also known as the Martini trophy – with three men at the finish.

With Barbotin in between the two French groups, Bidot had a choice. Send him to support the Darrigade group and push harder for the stage win, or let him slip back to support the Bauvin group in which Géminiani and Malléjac are burning up matchsticks to keep Bauvin in the race. Who'd be a team director, he thinks to himself. Stick. Twist.

It was easier as a rider.

It's Bauvin, he shouts from the 203. Stay back and support Gilbert. We may need him.

Darrigade and the boys were counting off the kilometres in the meantime. 30km to go, 20km. The gap had stayed the same and remained the same at 10km to go. The roads had flattened, the pace had picked up both here and behind, the wind was at their backs. Toulouse – and Françoise – were waiting. When like a whip cracking at André's rear wheel, a tyre gave up its soul, puncturing at 8km from the finish.

Guys, help me out. Give me a wheel.

And so started the betrayal. Privat pretended not to notice. He rode on, leaving his friend and colleague stranded. Forestier would save me, thought André, Forestier's a good sort. But each to their own, thought Forestier, the 4CV is on its way, they'll sort you out André. They've got a spare wheel waiting for you, I'm off.

André's problem was that the 4CV was stuck behind Rolland and Bergaud still, a handful of kilometres further back. The 203 was further back with Bauvin, Malléjac, Géminiani and Barbotin. Who to turn to? A hopeless André stood alone at the side of the road brandishing his wheel. Each second that passed was a second lost in the General Classification, so André set about repairing the tyre himself.

Leaping back on his bike, Darrigade pumped at his pedals, trying to regain some of the pace he'd earned for his teammates who were perhaps already in the velodrome, perhaps already celebrating in front of Françoise, the bastards.

Bidot pulled alongside in the 203.

"What's going on? Where's Jean and René?"

"Fuck you Bidot. Fuck you and fuck your French team. They've buggered off without me haven't they."

"Easy André, I'm sure they had their reasons."

"Reasons? Fuck you and your reasons," screamed Darrigade, throwing the deflated spare inner tube through Bidot's open window. "And screw Bauvin."

Bidot's mistake? To have acted in support of men he thought under threat in the General Classification, and not to have acted in support of the man he thought a certainty for the stage win. In hedging his bets and believing that Gilbert Bauvin was the man to protect and bring back to the main group, Bidot had seen his other potential winner eliminated.

Darrigade rode into Toulouse to a hero's welcome. De Filippis's stage win was greeted with subdued enthusiasm, but Darrigade – the boy from the South – was received with a standing ovation worthy of a world champion.

He hardly noticed.

He was two minutes behind the stage winner, but effectively out of the running for the General Classification. Throwing his bike to one side, Darrigade sat crying by the railings, hurling insults at anyone who approached. Treason, he cried. I've been betrayed by my team, by Marcel, by fate. You're all bastards.

Françoise was advised to hold back, to leave André to himself, for now. After all, she's far too young to hear these things.

A relieved Gilbert Bauvin had only lost a couple of minutes. It could have been far worse, were it not for the efforts of Raphaël Géminiani and Jean Malléjac. And yet, that evening, it was Bauvin who provided Andre Darrigade with perhaps his biggest insult of the day:

"What was he hoping for? That he'd float over the Alps?"

Ah yes, Darrigade. Hopeful. Ambitious. Over-reaching himself, perhaps, but what's wrong with that? After all, he'd completed the Pyrenees, he'd tackled the Aspin, the Peyresourde, the Portet d'Aspet – and he was leading the team 8km out from the finish on the final Pyrenees stage. But tonight, no hope. No ambition. No more over-reaching himself.

André Darrigade's tour was over, and he'd return to the ranks, a hollowed-out shell of a man no longer quite himself, no longer enjoying the Tour, no longer competing for the Tour.

At least that would make Marcel Bidot's task a little easier.

Little Louis and the Breakawee
19th July 1956
Stage 14, Toulouse to Montpellier, 231km

P'tit Louis Decides

Louis Caput's career is coming to an end. Mind you, they've been saying that for several years and despite these regular proclamations, 'P'tit Louis' rode over 30,000km last year including all three Grand Tours and the 6 days of Paris at the end of the season, just to round things off and prove to everyone that Louis Caput was not kaput.

Louis had always been the boss of the peloton, whichever team he rode for. But rather than instilling fear into other riders around him, he instilled respect. When Louis Caput said ride, you rode, and you rode all day. He was clever, too. A brain that worked overtime, calculating average speeds and time gaps, knowing just when to push the button and release a breakaway, knowing who to let go, and knowing which men had their little deals – who was on the take, who was doped, who needed a helping hand. The peloton of the late 40s and early 50s was a Caput peloton, and it was all the better for it.

He was made for hard work – Louis was brought up on a farm in typical pre-war hardship, waking up at 3 every morning to milk the cows and then delivering the milk on his bike. For every rider, a unique story of hardship that built them into the man they are today. For Louis, there was no story of redemption, no rags to riches glory, there was just hard work and pleasure from it. He'd take the same attitude from the farm straight to the bike race, putting in the shifts.

And so, with age, P'tit Louis has become Le Professeur, a wise old sage within the cycling community. To emphasise his professorial acumen, Louis Caput has taken to spending more time with the Velo-Club Sannois, accompanying the young cycling graduates on training sessions. Perhaps fatherhood has played its part. His six-year-old son has already taken up cycling and regularly plays the 6 days of Paris with his friends. But not for 6 days, and not in Paris.

They say that Roger Hassenforder's form so far in this Tour can be put down to one man, and one man alone: P'tit Louis.

This is, let's not forget, the Roger Hassenforder that drove 'Tonin le Sage' (Antonin Magne) to distraction. The Roger Hassenforder who, just one year ago, drove his most loyal fans to distraction and wound up penniless at the end of a wretched, selfish season of showboating and capitulation.

In Pau, Caput commended Hassenforder on his performance in the mountains:

"So you see, you got over the Aubisque. Not so bad, is it? You just take a smaller gear, take your own time and you get there in the end."

"I'll get over all of them P'tit Louis. I'll definitely finish this Tour now. And you know what – I'm going to win more stages," beamed his pupil. "You'll see. We've already got 3 million francs in the bank. We'll have 5 by the time we reach Paris. They said they didn't want Hassen, well I'm showing them plenty of Hassen!"

Louis turned over in his bed, not wanting to show his protégé that he was smiling. Sometimes, however, you need to bring Hassen down from his cloud…

"You know what, the French cycling federation were right to punish you after what you did last year. There are some things a rider should never do. That cost you selection for the World Championships. Next time, you'll pipe down."

"You're right," nodded Hassenforder. "I was an idiot."

Caput nearly somersaulted on the bed. Roger Hassenforder is accepting his advice.

"And there's no reason you can't climb the Alps," he carries on. "You'll never climb like Charly Gaul, but do everything I ask of you and you'll finish this Tour. Stay by my side and don't look to hold on to guys who are going quicker than you. The only thing you need to do is get there before the cut-off. Make time up on the descent and you'll be OK."

Caput looked across. His student was already asleep. Student or friend? It's a curious friendship, he thought to himself.

And so, on the start line in Toulouse, Roger Hassenforder has ensured that he is behind P'tit Louis, who is dishing out instructions to the Bretons around him. Picot – wearing the green jersey after two successive second-place finishes in Luchon and Toulouse last night – is to watch the Belgians for their intentions and report back. Le Ber is told to get himself into any breakaway that happens – he'll try to keep the gap down for Hassen who will take things up later in the stage.

If all goes to plan, Caput says, then we'll be drinking champagne in Montpellier tonight.

Constantine's Error

The traditional skirmishes at the start of a stage are once more being marshalled by Stan Ockers, who has become domestique de luxe for Jan Adriaenssens, and now self-proclaimed hard man of the peloton.

Raymond Elena, the French-Algerian rider from the South-West team, breaks away and is told in no uncertain terms by Ockers that he is to return to the ranks right now, or find himself frozen out of any deals.

Elena's perhaps too young to understand the complexities of the 1950s peloton. When the world champion tells you to get back or lose your future bargaining power, generally speaking you withdraw.

But he pleads with Ockers – just let me go – I want to ride – and Ockers spends some time considering this. Does it matter if Elena goes? He's no threat to our yellow jersey, and what's more – letting him go would deprive Laurédi of a teammate when it comes down to a straight-out fight between Laurédi and Adriaenssens.

OK, you can go this time, concedes Ockers, and Elena is allowed to leap away like a rabbit freed from a trap.

This moment of lassitude is perhaps a misjudgement as others look ahead and see Raymond Elena distancing himself. Le Ber goes, just as P'tit Louis instructed him, and then off goes Wout Wagtmans – the Clown – and the Spaniard Bahamontes, along with a handful of other non-threatening riders. Stay close, says Caput, we'll form a chase group later, there's plenty of time to ride.

Ockers is forced to join the group himself, and the Belgians at the front of the peloton start to panic. This wasn't meant to happen. This wasn't part of the plan. Stan, bring them back. But Stan wouldn't bring them back, and Jan Adriaenssens found himself isolated in the chase.

Like a thread pulled at a sweater, the race was coming apart in front of his eyes.

Little Louis and the Breakawee

A Roger Hassenforder Type of Day

In front of Adriaenssens went three more riders, and one of them was Roger Hassenforder. Leave them, shouts Brankart, taking the role of Ockers in the main group. None of them matter.

The announcement of a chasing group had gone through the radios and had found its way onto the blackboards ahead of the lead group. Only 50km had been raced, and we are already 23 minutes ahead of schedule. With the Pyrenees left behind, the race is returning to Classics mode.

Behind, Adriaanssens shakes his head and digs deep. Only his teammates are willing to work with him, the others know that this is probably a Roger Hassenforder type of day and it's not worth chasing him down.

By 81 kilometres, the chase group has caught the breakaway and we now have a group of 18 men and a peloton that has largely given up the ghost. For Adriaenssens, it's a case of minimising losses against two men: Bahamontes and, of all people, the Dutchman Wagtmans. Who let him go up ahead? There are arguments within the team. Ockers is the man to blame, someone says, he let this happen. But you were meant to watch for escapees, shouts Desmet to no one in particular. But who would have thought of Wout Wagtmans at the start of the day? Indeed, in this Tour, who are you supposed to mark? Everyone's riding for themselves today, except for the Belgians.

The journalists have taken advantage of this entente to slow down and admire the scenery a little. Zaaf, the photographer, has forgotten his camera and has to report back to the Miroir des Sports car to convey the beauty of the scenery further down the road. The advantage, Zaaf adds, is that he can take the road less travelled, navigate the roadblocks in town centres and do a little tourism on the side. Sun-burnt hills, he reports. I'd retire here if I could. The real Midi, the beating heart of the south, a place where man has conquered rock – a wild land, replete with the sound of cicadas, the Orb valley in flower and its small parcels of land broken up by low stone walls, the scent of lavender... ahhh, Zaaf says, there's no camera that can capture the majesty of the Midi.

Very well, says Chassaignon, leaning out of the Peugeot. Beautiful words, but no photographs. I'll just have to add in a few more paragraphs.

Gaston Bénac proffers an imaginary coupe of Champagne towards the photographer-poet. The old man has a smaller column these days, but Zaaf has just added some colour.

Can I Not Have A Wazz?

In the front group, the instigator of the breakaway, Raymond Elena, has gone far enough without the call of nature. "I need to piss," he screams to his breakaway colleagues. "Can we have a wee break?"

"Piss off," shouts Dotto, to general laughter.

"Ah come on, can I not have a wazz?"

"We're not stopping," Dotto insists, "so piss on your bike or hold it until we get to Montpellier. Got that?"

Elena mopes. This was his breakaway and now they've stolen it from him. But he can't hold.

He stands while pedalling, one hand on the left handlebar, the other forcing his shorts up on the right-hand side, trying to find a gap for his member so that he doesn't piss in his shorts, but manages to find a way through, preferably without pissing on himself.

Warm piss splashes off the bike frame, half of it back onto Raymond's leg, the other half onto the road, with some splash going onto his shoes. Ah shit, he says, I'm going to stink. They'll never ride with me.

The call of nature, when it comes, lasts longer than it should. It always does when you need to move.

When Raymond looks up, they've gone 200 metres up the road. He stashes his cock back in his pants, wipes his hand on the back of his shorts and pumps hard down on the pedals, shouting at them – get back here, stop fucking with me, come on, I've done the work. I deserve this.

Nobody turns round. Elena's day is done, a piss too far.

Hassen and De Clown

Of the 17 men up ahead, six have found a little space by switching to the left-hand side of the road. Bahamontes is among them, so too is Wout Wagtmans and of course, Roger Hassenforder. Le Ber is with him and the two know full well that Hassen is the man to bring home the money. Stick to my wheel, he says. I'll ride you home. Hassenforder nods and rides his tailwind.

The top six enter the velodrome in Montpellier, and Federico Bahamontes gives the sign that he's not going to compete. Wagtmans goes first, the little man arching his back over his handlebars into the first corner. Game on, shouts Le Ber, pulling Hassenforder with him into fourth, then third place. De Groot, the Dutchman, takes over from his friend and colleague, hoping he'll latch on, but the Le Ber-Hassenforder combination is far faster, and Le Ber pulls off, allowing Roger Hassenforder to sprint for the line – a formality, in hindsight – but a majestic one for the man from Alsace who celebrates arms in the air, as the bank balance of the Breton team kerchings itself another notch higher.

The Dutch pair of De Groot and Wagtmans have taken

advice – the peloton is so far behind that a miracle might be happening. Wout Wagtmans might be in yellow tonight. Calculations are made. If the peloton doesn't arrive within 19 minutes, then Wagtmans is in yellow. Roger Hassenforder pokes his nose in between the two men as they study the roadmap once more on the grass.

"Reckon you're in yellow, Clown?"

"Dunno, Rog. They've stopped giving us the time gaps."

"You see Elena pissed himself?" he laughs, and they all laugh before Wout and his teammate return nervously to the road map. Remember this bit? That'll slow them down. And this bit here, that's fast. They'll make up time here. There's no purpose to this debating, other than to pass the time.

And time does pass, as it always does, just not enough for Wout Wagtmans to take the yellow he had barely dared dream of before today's stage. 18 minutes was the gap between the breakaway group and the peloton, 18 minutes of waiting for Wout until Jan Adriaanssens and his teammates, including the man who misread the whole stage, Stan Ockers, roll into the velodrome and compete for the peloton sprint.

Wout doesn't see who won it. He doesn't care. But he knows that while he's not in yellow tonight, he's as close as he has been thanks to Stan Ockers' marvellous mistake.

And this is a chance he doesn't want to pass up on.

The Physician, The Belgians, and the Fishy Excuses

20th July 1956
Stage 15, Montpellier to Aix-en-Provence, 204km

Dumas Doesn't Understand

Pierre Dumas is not a cycling man. Four years ago, when on holiday climbing in the Alps, a call came. The Tour physician is sick. No, he couldn't heal himself. Come quick.

Damn, thought Dumas. I don't care for cyclists. Or cycling.

And here he still is, bemused at the world of men riding their bikes and their injuries and their illnesses and – frequently – their drugs. Now, this is not to say that Pierre Dumas accuses the Belgian team of taking some form of drug, probably amphetamines, he would be unlikely to say. No, there's an honour that comes with being the Tour physician. You don't say these things out loud.

That's what everyone else is intimating. And Pierre Dumas doesn't have an answer to this, at least not an answer that he can say in public.

As Jan Vlaeyens, once loyal lieutenant to Ockers, Brankart, De Bruyne and then Adriaenssens, pulls out with dysentery (again, this is what Vlaeyens claims, and Pierre Dumas will neither deny nor confirm this), the Belgian day starts to go badly wrong. Or did it go wrong when Ockers and

Adriaenssens dropped down the peloton like two stones being thrown from a cliff?

Bad fish, they're saying. We all had the fish.

Ah, it's always the fish, murmurs Dumas. Always the fish.

And there's Brankart, throwing up over a stone wall. This was meant to be a simple stage, how am I meant to cure an entire team?

There was Malléjac of course, last year. He wasn't alone with his misadventures. You should have seen Ferdy Kübler, at his grand old age, steaming up the Mont Ventoux telling everyone including Gem himself that Ferdy is a grand champion, look at me go, Ferdy Grand Champion, and then they found him singing songs like a drunkard before falling over, grey-faced and sweating. Still pedalling.

Oh Ferdy, how could you.

Pills and Bottles

Dumas, he doesn't understand why cyclists do these things. He doesn't see the ageing Kübler fighting for one last hurrah, trying to keep up with the younger boys on Ventoux. He doesn't see Malléjac's need to be important. He doesn't see the constant scrabbling around for attention so that managers will pick riders for criteriums so that the photographers will find them in a breakaway, so that they can just keep up with the damn pace, always the damn pace, faster every year.

Dumas walks into the bedrooms at night after the soigneurs have gone and finds pills he hasn't prescribed himself. He finds bottles lying around that aren't for water, they could never just be for water. He finds soigneurs secretly squirrelling packages in bags, he finds managers whispering surreptitiously, but none of this means anything to Pierre. He's just here to treat the riders, and perhaps help them see the error of their ways.

He gives Vlaeyen a disapproving look. Dysentery, you say. Is it, my boy. Well, come with me, drink plenty of water. We'll sort out your "dysentery".

Dumas is unaware that fish was not even on the menu at the Belgians' hotel last night. They couldn't even be bothered to make up a proper excuse. Do some groundwork.

He doesn't really care, he just wants the riders to stop this nonsense before one of them is killed. Did they not see what drugs did to Hugo Koblet? The handsome Swiss climber, he'd have dominated cycling for ten years, were it not for some quack insisting he take an injection. And for what? To finish his national Tour and please the sponsors.

Cycling, he muses, is populated by juju men, shamans, charlatans. And these riders, young men all of them, they fall for it. For what? A few centimes more and their face on the front of l'Equipe?

So, as we bid goodbye to the Belgians, and specifically the yellow jersey of Adriaenssens, to what do we owe this particularly ill-fated alleged drug-taking? Yesterday's chaos which saw the yellow jersey lead cut while Wout Wagtmans managed to chisel back an 18-minute deficit? The increasing menace of the Spaniard Federico Bahamontes, a similar deficit behind with the Alps to come? Or the regularity of Roger Walkowiak, constantly in the GC bunch with barely a bead of sweat on his forehead? Whatever the reason, the Belgians saw fit to allegedly take some form of doping ahead of a flat stage that should really never have caused them a problem, and this ahead of a rest day, too.

There really was panic among the Belgian camp last night, and today they're pedalling squares, vomiting in fields and looking, to those who know these things, like the team that got a duff supply of amphetamines.

Were they aware? Or were they, like Kübler and Malléjac,

supposedly taken by surprise that their manager had slipped them a wrong'un in their bidon? It's not unheard of, but it's almost unheard of for a member of the peloton these days not to be on something. And given the pace of this Tour, it's almost unreasonable to expect that they're riding on spring water.

And what a shame for Jan Adriaanssens, the trainee boulanger who was never meant to wear yellow. He was brought up in Antwerp to rise early, work hard and earn a crust, if you'll pardon the pun. He chose cycling after discovering that he could get home quicker after a long stint at the bakery, but moreover, he chose cycling because he wanted to sleep normal hours like the rest of us. He wanted to be normal.

And normal he was. A man born to servitude within the peloton, "Solid Jan", they'd call him – Sterke Jan. Solid Jan would carry water, fetch the sugared beer when he was asked to, he'd shield Ockers and Brankart from the wind, he'd pull De Bruyne to the finish line. Solid Jan, the man whose yellow jersey meant so much to him that he couldn't finish telling his mother over the phone that he'd taken the lead in the Tour de France. He just broke down in tears, his voice halting.

Not so solid Jan, then.

And he's crying as he, together with the rest of the Belgium team, keep turning the wheels, each up-stroke a stab to the back, each down-stroke a stab to the heart, each pothole in the road forcing the stomach to turn, a retching rushing up the throat, but no – carry on. It was the fish. Tell everyone it was the fish.

Tears of the Clown

Whatever it was, it appears to have gone through Ockers' system as he leaps from one group to the next, leaving the sick Adriaanssens to his fate.

The Physician, The Belgians, and the Fishy Excuses

Perhaps it was the salty air of the Camargue wafting over the peloton, or the scent of lavender that put juice into Ockers' engine? Perhaps it was the Mistral, one of its more tender days, giving a helpful push where it was required most. Perhaps it was the surprise climbs of the Alpilles, the mini-Alps of Provence, pushing Stan Ockers back to his limits, reminding him to ride and ride hard.

This is France at its most overwhelming. Not a day to be sick, thinks Ockers. Get over it.

The stage itself is a series of attacks on the Belgians. Siguenza was allowed to go ahead and soak up a little Languedocquien adoration early on, for he is from those parts. He was then reeled back in with a hasty "had your fun, boy", and spat out the back where he belongs.

Ockers, once recovered, couldn't follow the group of Forestier, Thomin, Barbotin and a group of regional riders looking to make their names, and lo and behold, it's a cinder track. So it's the Breton Thomin who wins the sprint – as everyone predicted the minute the group got away.

Thomin, adding to the Breton piggy bank on the kind of track he grew up on.

But neither Thomin nor Forestier are the story here. It's the little Dutchman with the huge smile and the tears of joy, who realises that his rival for the yellow jersey is way back, nine whole minutes back, and he's no longer just the virtual yellow jersey, he's the real deal.

Wagtmans whips out the cigars as the lead of the Tour passes from one low country to the next. A huge smile plays on his face as he's mobbed by teammates in orange.

Adriaenssens, when he makes it into the velodrome, is spent. Sterke Jan hauls his significant frame over his handlebars and watches the sweat drip from his forehead onto his front wheel. A bad day for the Belgians, a bad day for Adriaenssens, but if we're going to be honest about it, a bad day for cycling.

The problem is, nobody's going to be honest about it.

None The Wiser, Nothing By Half
21st July 1956
Rest Day, Aix-en-Provence

None the wiser, Nothing by half

There have been many yellow jerseys so far in this Tour de France, but as the race takes a break in Aix-en-Provence, the Alps loom large over the Tour and we're still none the wiser as to who will be riding yellow into Paris.

Wout Wagtmans is the latest wearer of yellow and is perhaps our most serious contender yet to have worn it. Wout can climb, he can time trial – and this will be handy with the time trial coming up after the Alps – and his slight frame belies a punchy strength that the beefier Belgians would be proud of. Wout's childhood is not out of place with many in the peloton. A farmhand at the age of 14 with parents eager to put him and his seven siblings to work as soon as possible, Wout discovered the bike, and discovered an easier way to make money.

Wout did nothing by half. As an amateur rider, he signed up for two simultaneous races, earning himself a suspension as well as a podium finish. He quickly turned professional and became the youngest ever Dutch rider in the Tour de France in 1950. Wout's problem, if it were a problem, was that he simply couldn't stop riding. He'd ride almost non-stop from March to November every year, and would then train 6 days a week in the winter.

None of this would prevent Wout Wagtmans from living the life he'd dreamed of. He bought a house for his parents and more for his relatives and friends. He'd buy new cars – American or German – whichever was fastest. You'd find Wout in the nightclubs of Paris, you'd find him smoking cigars and drinking whisky. You'd even find him drinking mid-race. Wout lives life as fast as he rides his bike, and today in Aix-les-Bains, the little Dutchman the peloton loves and knows as The Clown, is finally able to rest, and rest in a yellow jersey at that.

Does anyone take his claims seriously? Could he really hold on to yellow all the way to Paris? Wagtmans is a climber, slight of frame and a demon on the descent, and yet he isn't taken seriously. There is a suspicion that he'll crack in the Alps, a victim of his own hectic schedule.

Louison Loves Laurédi

Breathing down his neck is the man Louison Bobet loves to hate – Nello Laurédi. Nello hasn't really disturbed anyone during this Tour. He has sat in behind wheels, rarely challenged for finishes, but has displayed a rather boring tendency to be consistently there or thereabouts, finding himself on the second rest day with around 90 seconds'C deficit on the yellow jersey and his favourite mountains about to spring up from the earth in front of them. Three-time winner of the Dauphiné Liberé, Laurédi is even being taken seriously by Bobet himself.

The Bobet-Lauredi rivalry dates back to 1953 when Nello won a stage in a sprint ahead of Bobet, who was aiming for the first of his three Tour victories. Louison was still usually called Louis at that stage – a nervous, spindly individual with bags of promise, but a palmarès waiting to be written. Bobet confronted Laurédi after the race, and the French team appeared to be siding with their Franco-Italian friend and not Bobet. All of that changed when the team leader agreed to share his winnings with the team. Nello Laurédi had won not just the stage, but he had boosted his own personal finances that day.

In a straight-up duel between Wagtmans and Lauredi, the romantic follower of the Tour might side with Laurédi. Rejected by the French national team, Nello now finds himself in one of the worst regional teams around, Sud-Est. Apart from Jean Dotto – himself excluded from the French national team even after having won the Vuelta last year – the team is made up of allegedly hapless, disorganised and ill-disciplined riders including the former lanterne rouge Raymond Meyzenq who somehow found the legs to climb the mountains with the best of them before falling back into the ranks where he belongs.

So if Nello Laurédi is to win this Tour, it's without the help of teammates, unlike Wagtmans who can count on Nolten, Van der Pluym and Voorting among others.

A Picot In The Tour

Journalists are quick to avoid the name of Fernan Picot, even though the Breton is wearing green and is bringing home more money to the Ouest team than multiple stage-winner Roger Hassenforder.

There are more glitzy names in the Breton cohort.

Fernan Picot is another of those riders nobody expected to crest the Pyrenees, and yet crest them he did, finishing 2nd behind Jempy Schmitz on the breakaway day and then second again. Picot keeps popping up, and yet like Roger Walkowiak, he's rarely considered a threat despite his consistency. And consistency wins tours.

Picot is young, and green is perhaps the best jersey he could hope for with the Alps ahead of him, which should prove too stern a challenge for the Breton. Antoine Blondin called him a little pocket picker for the way in which he nicked races from some of the bigger fellows in the pack such as Mahé. His teammates called him Frog's Legs, something to do with his riding style; you can imagine what they might be implying.

He made his name beating Fritz Schär, the Swiss ratagasse, two years ago. That got peoples' attention, but he was overlooked for the Tour with Tour organiser Jacques Goddet famously saying "We'll have no Picots on this Tour". This was not – it should be said – about Fernan, but about the illegal nougat sellers found ambling among the crowds at start and finish towns, also known as Picots. It's Goddet's Tour, and he will control everything, especially the commercial aspects.

Either way, it rankled with Fernan, who trained harder that winter to ensure that there would be at least one Picot on the Tour.

This year, his first at Mercier, he is playing an altogether different game – more patient, dare one say it – better managed.

Admire Cézanne, Roger

And then, of course, there is Roger Walkowiak. The Nord-Est-Centre man doesn't have a team of luxury domestiques around him, but he does have the experience of Adolphe Deledda and the inspired leadership of team director Sauveur Ducazeaux. Roger got in the famous breakaway alongside

Fernan Picot and multiple others on the road to Angers, but Roger has been in breakaways and chasing groups for most of the race, except when in yellow. He was in the original Darrigade breakaway on stage 1 until he punctured, and he climbed the Pyrenees with consummate ease.

Ducazeaux has been transformed as a technical director, too. From the easy-going régionale coach, Ducazeaux has morphed into a strategist with military precision, dosing each meal and every bidon with just the right amount of nutrition required, ensuring his men sleep the precise number of hours per night required. Ducazeaux may not have the army he would have wanted, but he has the battle he has longed for all his life.

Today, Ducazeaux has chosen to take Walkowiak to the art gallery. Take his mind off the race, at least temporarily. They're putting on a special Cézanne exhibition, and half the caravane is there to appreciate it.

50 years since he died, boy, 50 years, can you believe it. How apt that the Tour should stop off here, at the home of Cézanne, after having ridden through those sun-bleached fields of Provence, through towns of white-washed houses and fields of lavender. Dear boy, I know you don't look up from your handlebars, but you have one day to admire the work of this man, one day.

He's impressed by his rider's sang-froid and the relaxed manner in which he has adapted to the role of hunter for the yellow jersey. He has climbed well in the Pyrenees and he claims openly that if his man can maintain his place ahead of the crucial Gap-Turin stage, then the race is as good as won.

For now, Ducazeaux says, admire Cézanne. Your time will come.

Dotto and Lerda leave Laurédi in the lurch
22nd July 1956
Stage 16, Aix-en-Provence to Gap, 203km

The Alps? Today?

The Belgians needed the rest day perhaps more than anyone else. It is spoken in the corridors of the team hotels that fish was most definitely not on the menu that night, and indeed the Belgians got a 'bad batch'. Shaken by their performance the previous day, someone appeared to have called in supplies, and Jan Adriaenssens took it badly.

Looking at Fred De Bruyne on the start line at Aix-en-Provence, you may have thought that the 'bad fish' was causing a hangover of sorts. The Classics man is furiously tinkering with his bike after discovering that today is an Alpine stage and not a flat stage as he had thought.

Most riders will spend the evening reading the Tour roadbook, an essential guide to each stage detailing every twist and turn. Back in the day, Eugène Christophe, he of broken forks fame, used to note down every day's itinerary as it was written in L'Auto so that he wouldn't get caught out. But never did The Old Gaul discover on the start line that he was unexpectedly heading out into the mountains. Schoolboy error.

New wheels are called for, as De Bruyne fiddles with his saddle height for what is now, it seems, a tougher day than he bargained for.

Nello's Idiots

9km outside of Aix-en-Provence, the now customary breakaway makes its break. As is now routine in this most erratic of Tours, the breakaway appears to make no tactical sense. Dotto and Lerda, two teammates of Nello Laurédi, have found themselves caught up in the action and have steamed off ahead with a group of others, much to the confusion of team leader Laurédi, whose yellow jersey ambitions had been growing by the day.

Laurédi pulls up alongside the team car and demands to know what his teammates are doing. He is met with shrugs and a general "just let it play itself out", but Laurédi has been around long enough to know the risks of letting two teammates get so far ahead. One would be plenty.

With them are Van Genechten, one Belgian who appears to have read the racebook ahead of the day's racing, as well as Forestier, Baffi, Nolten, Barbosa and Audaire. A high-quality breakaway yet one that poses absolutely no threat to the yellow jersey or any of its pretenders, a list that we can start to whittle down as we reach the Alps.

These are the men most likely:

- Nello Laurédi – unusually circumspect, but consistent
- Gilbert Bauvin – has the weight of the French team behind him
- Wout Wagtmans – current yellow jersey holder, and he can climb
- Federico Bahamontes – if he can claw back some time in

the Alps, he is the world's best climber after all
- Roger Walkowiak – ever-present, although he would have to do it all alone
- Gerrit Voorting – former yellow jersey, and known for his climbing ability
- Jan Adriaenssens – Solid Jan had the 'bad fish' episode, but showed in the Pyrenees that he could match the climbers

The contenders all find themselves together in a pleasing entente. The time will come to attack, but today is all about getting to the Izoard in one piece. Time, then, to enjoy the lavender-coated foothills of the Alps, the gorges and the rocky precipices, the streaming rivers and the Marquis de Sade's house, somewhere up in that barren hill over there. Would any of the riders have known that?

Unlikely, but old Gaston Bénac has marked his racebook down with that one.

The riders have passed through the Lubéron with its perched villages, lavender valleys and its Mistral, and are entering the foothills of the Alps.

Bahamontes Breaks Free

Those Alps, then. They've been rising into view all day. What started as bumps on the horizon has quickly transformed into rocky walls and the first ascents of the day.

We start with the Col du Pointu, which, as it turns out, is not very pointu, and the Col du Croix de l'Homme Mort which, as it turns out, doesn't have any dead men on it. Nor any crosses.

That said, Nello Laurédi is beginning to wonder whether he is the homme mort in question. He was powerless to respond to a break out of the peloton from number four in our list, Bahamontes, drafted in the slipstream of two of his colleagues, Lampre and Lorono. Whether Laurédi should have been alert to the break or not is hardly the question. Whether his teammates should have been around him to bring the break to heel or not – well, that's a question we can't ask of them, as two were in the breakaway.

Idiots, thinks Laurédi.

By the time the original break had reached the Col du Croix de l'Homme Mort, Bahamontes was alongside them.

Dotto and Lerda looked at each other, each one realising what they had done.

"Shit. He's a player."

What Bahamontes and his two compadres had done was nothing short of miraculous. They had bridged a gap of 8 minutes between peloton and breakaway, roughly in the space of 15km. As the group takes the descent of the second climb of the day, Bahamontes welcomes the opportunity to freewheel and take as much of a ride home as he possibly can. If he can keep his 8-minute gap over Laurédi and the others aiming for yellow, Bahamontes will climb the general classification significantly.

Forestier's Promise

However, it's Jean Forestier who is causing journalistic pens to scribble furiously. First over the not very pointy Pointu, Forestier took all of the mountain points of the Homme Mort as well, before taking on the col de la Sentinelle and taking all three available points there, too. Not that Forestier is any challenger to Valentin Huot, King of the Pyrenees at the very least, on 26 points – Forestier started the day on 3, and would end it on 12 points, but he would end the day very much with his reputation bolstered.

Dotto and Lerda leave Laurédi in the lurch

This is Forestier's third Tour, and his third as a tricolore. Whereas most riders would start their careers working their way up through regional teams, Forestier earned selection for the French national team in just his third year as a pro, supporting Louison Bobet's second Tour win in '54. The young tricolore had underlined that early promise by winning Paris-Roubaix in '55 and earlier this year, winning the Ronde van Vlaanderen ahead of Ockers and Van Steenbergen.

Today, Forestier is making a name for himself. This boy is one for the future.

Forestier's immediate future is the descent into Gap, one taken at a furious pace as his breakaway companions Baffi and Barbosa appear the most likely to challenge for the sprint which will take place at the bottom of the Sentinelle.

As per the order of the day so far, it is indeed Forestier who wins the sprint – not that Baffi and Barbosa are much of a match for him, but it's Bahamontes who keeps the keenest eye on the time. The boards have been consistently giving him an 8-minute lead over the peloton, and as Forestier washes, combs à la Koblet and takes his first interviews, Bahamontes is in deliberation with his breakaway colleagues about just how much he has eaten into the GC leaders' advantage.

Dotto and Lerda are equally not so keen to see the arrival of the peloton, and the inevitable castigation they would receive from Laurédi. They know they've exposed their teammate today. They've given Bahamontes a target and have left Laurédi vulnerable.

With the Izoard on the menu for tomorrow, Dotto and Lerda have just made it harder for everyone.

The Revival of Charly Gaul, and the Man Who Wasn't There
23rd July 1956
Stage 17, Gap to Turin, 234km

"The Tour de France is over. Now we've got a Six Day race…"

Roger Hassenforder

Welcome to Izoard

Roger Hassenforder is not often quoted as a Tour de France sage. More of a goon, even though 1956 is proving to be a turning point for the man from Sausheim. And he's right, in a way. The preliminaries are, at least, over. With only 6 days of racing left, we are effectively starting anew. A fresh challenge awaits – that of the Alps and notably the Izoard.

Izoard is a fearsome – and feared – climb. The highest point of this year's Tour comes early in the stage, perhaps too early, but is followed by Sestrières on the run-in to Turin, which will give the GC contenders plenty to think about in terms of tactics.

For Sauveur Ducazeaux and Roger Walkowiak, there are no teammates that can help in the Alps. It's very much a case of managing time gaps and sticking to the wheels of the right men. Bahamontes is a useful foil, suggests Ducazeaux.

He's right in between King of the Mountains and General Classification, so he'll be there for all the important breaks.

For Walkowiak, Ducazeaux has prepared two bidons with orange juice and rice. Ducazeaux is a restaurateur, and if he has learned anything about preparing for a race, it is that food matters. Grilled meat, mineral water and very little else is served at the table in the evening. And above all, he warns the riders, do not drink during the race.

If you accept water from the crowd, take it – they have been waiting all day for you, it will mean a lot to them. But use it to cool yourself. Use it to wet your lips but no more than that. Do not drink.

Today's early breakaway features 9 men, notably Valentin Huot who wants to mop up as many of the mountain points as he can before Charly Gaul finds his form. If Charly Gaul ever finds his form. Within the breakaway, Huot is joined by Robinson, Close, Jean Dotto (once more) and a handful of others who would have no bearing on the result, including two as yet unknowns – Siguenza and Mirando.

Mirando is another of Nello Laurédi's teammates, incapably stepping in for the hapless Lerda after yesterday's double breakaway, leaving the yellow jersey contender to fight in vain against attacks from Bahamontes and his team. With two men once more in the breakaway ahead of the Izoard, you would forgive Nello Laurédi for thinking that he doesn't have a team at all.

Mirando pretends not to be dreaming of glory for himself, and is currently trying to slow the break down, preventing Siguenza from riding off the front. An argument has developed. At first, it's handbags at dawn – a few mediterranean gestures, a shrug of the shoulders, a couple of curse words, and Mirando lashes out.

Siguenza thinks better of responding, but looks across to

The Revival of Charly Gaul, and the Man Who Wasn't There

the director's car which has pulled up like the mysterious teacher in the playground who always knows when a fight is likely to break out. Pointing at his temple, Siguenza suggests that Mirando is mad. Mirando suggests that Siguenza is something unprintable, and the episode is best forgotten.

Behind, Raphaël Géminiani has decided to break from the peloton in an attempt to catch the 9 escapees. It's perhaps the first time we've seen 'Top Gun' make any kind of move this year. After complaining to Louison Bobet about the first 9 stages, "Gem" has accepted that this year – like every year – is not going to be his year, and has taken on the mantle of also-ran. He was never in great shape anyway, and without Louison, he was downbeat.

As the riders pass between two walls of granite, the landscape begins to morph from one scene to another. The climbing has started and the Arvieux is the first opportunity for mountain points – mountain points that Valentin Huot mops up with disregard for his 9 companions. From Arvieux, the hairpins lead to Izoard, and Huot can start to look down on his breakaway buddies, their silver bikes shining like fish in the bright sunlight of a cloudless day.

Further below, if he cared to notice, Huot would have seen the first skirmishes between the yellow jersey groups. Adriaenssens has time to make up after stage 15's défaillance, and is followed by his teammate Stan Ockers. Bahamontes is on Ockers' wheel and right behind him is Walkowiak who has Gaul in close pursuit.

Once more, the landscape morphs from the green trees and tufts of grass to the casse déserte, the sand-brown, oppresive, glacial peak. From down below, the air is burning hot today, but up in the casse, Huot feels the freshness on his face, the sweat starting to chill. He feels the encouragement of the crowd, in parts several people deep and now closing in on him, running alongside, pushing him and breathing their winey breath in his face, hurling themselves alongside the new King of the Mountains.

As Huot dips, the crowds thin almost instantly, and he takes a newspaper to thrust down his jersey. It gets warmer down at the bottom, but it gets colder as you ride downhill.

The crowds have over 1'40" to wait for Bahamontes and Ockers, and five seconds behind them is Roger Walkowiak, riding effortlessly and calmly, finding a cadence and a rhythm that better riders might envy. Gaul is about 20 seconds behind him, and Adriaenssens is weakening.

Laurédi is starting to see his yellow jersey ambitions fall like rocks from the Izoard. With each push, Laurédi sees lesser men accelerate beyond him and he tucks his chin into his chest, focuses on the metre in front of him and gives in, gently. The gap grows between Gaul and Laurédi, and for his own sake, the man with the blackboard quietly retires from view.

Back up front, the descent has seen the men come back together, and around 15 have formed a group to get a better look at each other. Walkowiak, insouciant, looks the freshest, his small eyes like raisins in a snowman, staring straight ahead, focused on the backs of his prey, Ockers and Bahamontes.

As the Izoard turns from rocks to hairpins and eventually to forest, a sharp turn as the road flattens out takes a few riders by surprise. Walkowiak's back wheel juts out and a crunching sound is quickly followed by a fall. Instinct takes over. He quickly pulls on the steel brakes and manages the fall, but the wheel is broken. Ockers and Bahamontes have gone, hardly at a great pace as they haven't noticed.

Ducazeaux is quickly on the scene with the spare wheel, fetched from the back of the Peugeot. He is everything a Technical Director needs to be in a moment of crisis like this. Quiet, assured. Nothing is wrong here. We'll fix the wheel, you go chase those two. Dust yourself down. Take a breather. Ready? Interally, Ducazeaux is doing somersaults, reassuring himself that all will be well, that Roger is fine, that the bike is fine, there are no further technical issues here. All is well.

And thankfully, all is well. Walkowiak is back on the bike, and from now on, he would ride with a little more prudence.

Le Jeune Vieux

Charly Gaul is looking healthier, and as the descent into Briançon turns abruptly into a climb, he follows the attack of Valentin Huot as if seized by instinct.

Huot is good, though. Gaul fails to latch on to his wheel and only a regional rider called Le Guilly is able to go with him. With Sestrières still to come, Gaul realises that it's worth keeping something in the tank while Huot empties his.

This is Mont Génèvre, the penultimate climb of the day and beyond the peak is Italy. From the rugged, pointy, threatening climb of the Izoard, we are entering what you might term the Pyrenean Alps. A calmer scenery unfolds before our riders. The grass grows greener, the bumps roll more gently. Huot ascends peacefully and realises, in these Italian lands, that he has finally emptied his tank and Charly Gaul is on his back, at long last. He has hunted him down all afternoon and finally, Huot gives up the ghost. Not before taking all mountains points.

The journalists have a new name for Charly Gaul. Le Jeune Vieux, they have called him. The young oldie. He rides like a man from yesteryear. A pre-war rider in modern clothes. Look at him, cries Chassaignon to Bénac. Look at him go, dancing on his pedals. He's looking back to see the gap. He sits. He stands. He's beautiful.

Gaul, hero of the Giro, miraculously finds his feet the

minute the Tour crosses the border into Italy. It was obvious, if you think about it.

This is Sestrières and half of Italy has climbed the mountain to witness Charly Gaul, the man they've claimed as their own, climb mountains as other men breathe air. Effortless, angelic, serene, this is vintage Gaul already, the jeune vieux stretching even further ahead the chasing group, which includes Ockers, Bahamontes, Walkowiak. Three minutes, now four minutes, and the peak is marked by the Albergo Duca D'Aosta, a cylindrical hotel that has none of the aesthetic glory of the Izoard, none of the pleasure you would receive from witnessing the Chapel at the end of a hard climb up the Kapelmuur in Geraardsbergen. It is white as snow, and as ugly as hell.

Gaul leaves it behind and believes from the team cars that only Ockers and Bahamontes are in his wake, and indeed that they are many minutes behind. As the Luxemburger drops towards the plains that lead to Turin, he knows that he has 80km to survive if he is to win the stage, and even with the lead he has built up on Sestrière, this is unlikely.

What he doesn't know is that Ockers and Bahamontes are joined by 13 others in a sort-of-peloton that has grown in size and has grown in speed, and together they are tackling the hairpins that are carelessly strewn down the side of the mountain with Gaul in full view, if not immediately within catching distance. But catch they shall, and together into Turin they shall ride.

And so it is, with 20km left to ride, for those of a romantic disposition, one of the moments of the Tour.

Gaul is caught. Hauled back into the group, Gaul receives a few nods and, from the Italian riders, not very much at all in the way of acknowledgement. But one man recognises Gaul's effort, and that one man is Roger Walkowiak. He puts an arm around Gaul, and says:

"Come, Charly. Ride with us."

It's a rare moment of warmth in this do-or-die, stab-or-be-stabbed Tour de France. An opportunity for one rider to put aside the contest for a while and treat his fellow competitor as a human being. For all the cruel words spoken of Roger Walkowiak by the press and the fans alike so far during this race, this offers proof that Walkowiak is not just a good bike rider, but also a good man.

And so, as the peloton enters the Community Stadium in Turin, does its traditional lap around the velodrome in front of 10,000 people, most of whom work for FIAT, and most of whom have been given the day off by their kind bosses, does it really matter who wins this stage? For the record, it is local hero Nino Defilippis, but does that matter at all?

You may argue that Valentin Huot won the stage. At least, if you're counting the number of mountain-top finishes. Or you may argue that Charly Gaul won the stage, if you're awarding stages for elegance and sheer natural ability.

The Man Who Wasn't There

Or, you may argue that the true winner of this stage – and this is the direction in which the journalist community is heading – is one who barely broke sweat while ensuring that he stayed with some of the world's finest climbers. This man, Roger Walkowiak, rode nearly the perfect stage, carefully managing his opponents, carefully matching their every stride and carefully managing his time gaps. He has seen Laurédi flop, Wagtmans in yellow has lost time, Adriaenssens too. Roger did just what he did in the Dauphiné last year, even though nobody noticed him matching Bobet all the way – their eyes were all on Louison. He climbed majestically.

Quietly. In a manner that is entirely Roger Walkowiak. No fuss, no fireworks. Just a quiet efficiency.

Walkowiak is now 2nd in the Tour de France, and people have started to take note.

Sauveur Ducazeaux watches Walkowiak take the plaudits from his teammates when they arrive. Deledda is the first to shake his hand. Scodeller next.

And he is more certain than ever that Roger Walkowiak is going to take yellow tomorrow, and that he is going to win the Tour de France.

Suddenly, Ducazeaux is no longer alone in this point of view. In his personal diary, Jacques Goddet writes the following:

"What impressed me most was his calm, the ease with which he rode today. I asked Jacques Marchand, Tour de France correspondant with L'Équipe, to run with Walkowiak as his headline tomorrow morning. Everything must be about Walkowiak. This Tour has proven that he can ride with the greatest of riders, and he is capable of being a star. But also, Jacques must emphasise the fact that Walkowiak's performance puts the spotlight on those men who have served their time, and who have served the sport of cycling. Our task is to reveal the personality as yet unknown of a 29-year-old man who has taken on all of the great races, and now stands on the precipice of his greatest result."

That night, in his Turin hotel, Roger Walkowiak studies himself once more in the mirror. He makes a circle with his head, stretching his neck muscles, as Sauveur Ducazeaux sits back on the single bed, racebook in hand.

"It's between Turin and Grenoble that you're going to win this Tour", he asserts. "You'll attack. You'll put everything you've got into this one."

Walkowiak smiles.

"I'm saying nothing," he responds. "But I do believe I can

The Revival of Charly Gaul, and the Man Who Wasn't There

do it."

In a phrase, we have found the essence of Roger Walkowiak. A quiet confidence. A man whose personal quest may not have been long in the making, but a man who has found a new confidence.

No fuss, no fireworks.

This is a man who prefers gardening to nightclubs. While Wout Wagtmans is out partying, you'd likely find Walkowiak sitting by the lake, line fishing.

Perhaps we have all been tricked. Perhaps Roger Walkowiak was our Tour winner all along, and we just never noticed. We were taken in by his rosy red cheeks, his country boy appearance, his lack of a palmarès. But we forgot the Dauphiné. We ignored the fact that he's now 29 and reaching his peak. We forgot the breakaway to Angers. Our gaze was averted. We were watching Louison in '55, we were watching Charly Gaul today. On the road to Angers, we were watching André Darrigade.

Roger Walkowiak has pulled off the greatest trick of all – to convince us that he didn't even exist.

The Attack They All Missed
24th July 1956
Stage 18, Turin to Grenoble, 250km

A Time To Say Goodbye

There comes a time in every Tour to say goodbye. Yesterday, we said goodbye rather early on in the proceedings to Nello Laurédi, who was sharply and unceremoniously returned to the middling ambitions of the peloton. Today, everyone is certain that we'll be saying goodbye to Wout Wagtmans.

As the peloton leaves Turin, Wagtmans is sweating more than usual. Finally, it seems we have found 'the stage too far' for our Dutch friend, and it appears to be only a matter of time before the yellow jersey has to give up his maillot, at least virtually.

Sauveur Ducazeaux knows this, and he is eager to inform Roger Walkowiak, who is as usual hidden in the wheels of the climbers. The peloton has, for once, opted to stay together and there is no room for team cars to pull alongside their men yet.

We have three Alpine climbs today – the col du Mont-Cenis, which stands at 2,038m, the col de la Croix-de-Fer at 2,087m, and the Luitel which is minuscule at just 1,235m.

It is at the foot of the Mont-Cenis that things start to

develop, finally. Bahamontes is followed by the little Belgian Van Genechten, and the man who seeks the cold, Charly Gaul. That's the order in which they pass over the summit, but the developments further down the mountain are causing ripples. Wagtmans, as expected, is being pushed by his teammates. The Clown is in no mood for joking around today, he is shaking his head, flicking beads of sweat into the faces of his fellow riders.

This is one hill too many.

Gaston's Curse

André Chassaignon and Gaston Bénac have been admiring the scenery of the entre-deux-cols from the back of their car, but a technical problem means their radio has broken. They pull into St. Jean-de-Maurienne for lunch with one of the Tour dignitaries, a Mr Pierre Ruais from Paris.

"What's his name again?" enquires Bénac, never one for a non-cyclist.

"Ruais, Gaston. And eat quickly, will you?"

Bénac is a journalist fast going out of style, and he knows it. His era ended with the war. The era of the Maes brothers, Speicher, Magne and Leducq, the era of inner tubes around the shoulders and of goggles over the eyes, an altogether slower, grittier era than the athletic dynamism of the '50s. But Bénac is not given to Leducq-esque reminiscing. Cycling is a feast, and a feast takes on many courses, each to be savoured in its own way. The Pélissiers provided him with his starter, the Maes brothers his main course, and for pudding, Bartali, Coppi, Bobet and the two K's from Switzerland.

We're into digestif territory here, and Bénac has had a hearty meal.

The food arrives, quicker than in most towns, and the three

men give a hearty gallic welcome to the plates of chicken leg, pommes dauphinoises and green beans.

"So Monsieur Raisu," chews Bénac, intentionally getting the name wrong, "do you know who went over the Croix-de-Fer first?"

"As a matter of fact, I do. But you'll never guess who it was."

Chassaignon interjects. "It must be Lampre. Or Guitard. One of those boys. Yes?"

Ruais shakes his head, flecks of daupinoise sauce dropping from his beard. "Nn-hn," he utters. "You're nowhere near."

The dignitary smiles a smug smile. I know and they don't, it says.

He's ready now. "Hassenforder."

"Fuck right off!" shouts Bénac, dropping his fork in the process.

The smug look turns to appalled horror. They've heard old Bénac can be a bit fruity. Some of the other diners have recoiled in shock as well. They probably don't hear many curses in St. Jean-de-Maurienne.

"Get back in the car," yells Chassaignon, already heading for the exit. Another bill unpaid, forwarded to Miroir des Sports. Bénac apologises, makes his excuses, and waddles after his more agile colleague who is already in the car.

They race through the back markers and take several risks around tighter bends than their car can usually handle, flying past surprised riders before finding Hassenforder who is joking around with a few breakaway compatriots.

"Bravo! Roger, Bravo! What you're doing is magnificent!"

"Magnificently tiring, though!" beams Hassenforder.

"Whatever, you've excelled yourself."

"I had a bet with Caput that I could distance him!" yells the over-excited cyclist.

"Well you won, he's miles back!"

WALKO

The Attack They Missed

While Chassaignon and Bénac are celebrating Hassenforder's bet, they're missing perhaps the most important move of the day. Roger Walkowiak has attacked.

The man who wasn't there has silently launched his claim for the yellow jersey, distancing all but Gaul and Ockers who have latched on to his back wheel, but they aren't challenging for the yellow jersey. The attack is the final nail in the coffin for Wout Wagtmans who now finds himself five minutes behind Walkowiak on the day, and the descent of the Croix-de-Fer is taken at breakneck speed.

The French have an expression for a descent like this. They call it a descente à tombeau ouverte. An open-tombed descent. It's a frightening drop, but Walkowiak has wings. Nose into the wind, the new virtual yellow jersey is doing everything that Ducazeaux has asked of him. No longer managing every ounce of effort, Walkowiak is giving everything he has – emptying the fuel tank.

So when Gaul and Ockers detach themselves from the tiring Walkowiak, it barely matters. The job is done, and the yellow jersey – should he hang on – is his. Finally. And as promised. He tells himself to ignore the two climbers, and to focus on keeping a cadence, beating the tiredness that is now infiltrating his lungs, spreading through his legs, eating its way into his feet. A pain the like of which he hasn't experienced in this Tour so far, the pain of an extended effort, of a concerted attack.

The Luitel, supposedly minuscule, feels harder than the Croix-de-Fer, and the wind is now in Walkowiak's face. Like a boxer who has taken upper cut after upper cut, the man from Montluçon keeps rolling with the punches, slugging against himself, and yet he still rides.

Ducazeaux would protect his rider from the wind, were it from the side. Team cars have their uses. Instead, the Saviour leans out of the window and warns his rider not to put in an effort that might turn out to be fatal. For once, he is worried, although he takes care not to show it to his rider.

Walkowiak enters the Grenoble velodrome with Bahamontes and Nencini, a full nine minutes after Gaul, who eventually came in with over 3 minutes on Stan Ockers, which doesn't really matter, not in the big scheme of things. Walkowiak hauls his bike towards the central grassy area, leans against the metal barriers, and remains on his bike for several minutes. His eyes are red, his face haggard. Tears (once more) have formed at the corners of his eyes as the announcement goes out over the tannoy that he now leads the Tour de France officially.

The yellow jersey is back, on his back.

"It's over", proclaims Ducazeaux, arm around his back. "It's finished. You'll be wearing yellow in Paris, smoking your pipe."

Walko's Doubts

There has been a transformation today. Roger Walkowiak has become Walko. Newspaper headlines may have helped. It is easier to write Walko than it is to spell Walkowiak multiple times per report. And it helps French tongues get round the multiple non-native 'w' sounds.

And Walko could hardly not have noticed the encouragement of the crowds atop the Croix de Fer, the multiple shouts of "Allez Walko". Finally, some recognition.

However, Walko has doubts. The night is hot in Grenoble. The windows are open, and both Walko and Adolphe Deledda are still awake.

WALKO

"You know what," offers Walko into the silence. "If Marcel Bidot had picked me ahead of Lily Bergaud, I'd be Gilbert Bauvin's domestique. He'd be in yellow and I'd be an hour back. And now I've got four minutes on him. Almost."

Deledda offers a listening silence.

"He's got his teammates, and I've got nobody in the mountains. I'm always alone up there. But we've still got 815km to go. Four days… and I'm used to carrying water bottles. That's my job. I've always done it. I've never won a stage race."

Deledda acknowledges the monologue once more, in silence. The best counsellors do that, he thinks.

"Walkowiak, though. It's hardly the name of a great champion is it? It smells Polish. It doesn't sound right. It doesn't sound like a winning name like Bobet, Koblet, Kübler, Coppi…"

Deledda's not having this. "What about Kopa? Kopaszewski is even harder to pronounce than Walkowiak and yet we all called him Kopa, just as people called you Walko today. And remember, you've done everything right so far. You've been in the right breakaways, you've followed the right wheels, you attacked at the right moment. Nobody took you seriously, and here you are. Nothing will ever be the same again. Nobody will ever let you into another breakaway. You'll be marked like Ockers. This is the chance of your life, Roger. 800km to go and you can take this chance."

Doubts persist.

"Bauvin's got his teammates. So has Wagtmans. Adriaenssens too. I'm out there on my own."

Deledda doesn't take offence. He'll be there when Walkowiak needs him, so long as it's not up at the top of a major climb. He'll be there for the wheel changes he needs, he'll be up at 2 in the morning listening to Walko's doubts, and he'll be there in the morning with Walko's coffee.

The Crash, the Bandit, the Pursuit
25th July 1956
Stage 19, Grenoble to Saint-Etienne, 173km

Conjecture

While Walko has been having his doubts, there are others who – whisper it – are not convinced that he could, or even should, win the Tour de France.

Some reasons:

1. The man is a water-carrier who got lucky in a breakaway that nobody chased down.
2. Had Louison been racing, he would have been ten minutes ahead by now.
3. He hasn't even won a stage.

Conjecture, many might counter. And indeed, many are enthralled by the performance of Roger Walkowiak, as the crowds on the Croix-de-Fer yesterday will have demonstrated.

But aside from yesterday's attack against a man several minutes behind him, has there been a moment to define Roger Walkowiak's Tour? One that everyone will remember even fifty years from now? Ah…

WALKO

Cometh the moment

The stage from Grenoble to Saint-Etienne is not meant to trouble the leaders of the Tour unduly. With two climbs, the Oeillon and the Grand Bois, measuring just 1,434m and 1,160m respectively, with the last climb descending towards the finish line in Saint-Etienne, the stage is the last Alpine stage, and shouldn't carry much threat. It almost doesn't deserve the label 'Alpine'.

And yet… 112km into the stage, around Pélussin, Walkowiak is giving reason to his critics. He has settled into the middle of the peloton, rather than listening to the advice of Ducazeaux and Deledda, who have insisted that he ride prominently. The water-carrier has little experience of defending a yellow jersey, and has put himself at risk.

It's hard to say how the crash happened. A wheel touching another, a swerve from a régionale, a brake out of the blue. Who knows, but around thirty riders are caught up in a mangled, tangled mess of shining silver bike frames, legs and multi-coloured shirts. And shining bright in the middle of this morass of men – on the floor – the yellow jersey.

Immediately, the Nord-Est-Centre team react in shock. Bertolo and Chupin are caught up in the mess. Huyghe and Scribante stand by with their hands on their heads, caught in shock. Only the old head of Deledda is quick enough to react to the situation. In seconds, he is off his bike, hauling the yellow jersey out of the writhing remains of the crash, fixing the saddle and checking the wheels at high speed. Walkowiak is up, on his bike, and Deledda pushes with all his might, running alongside for a full ten seconds until Walkowiak is back up to full speed.

The commissaires have noticed, and have noted that Walkowiak will receive a penalty of 30 seconds.

The team is around Walkowiak, only for the yellow jersey's tyre to puncture almost instantly.

"Shit, Scodeller, give me your wheel – quick!" cries Walkowiak, visibly panicked. Another push from Deledda, this time away from the gaze of the commissaires who are furiously scribbling notes from the last incident, and Pierre Scribante pulls Walkowiak away for the chase.

The Chase

Gilbert Bauvin, then.

It had to be him.

Unshaven, wearing James Dean sunglasses, Gilbert Bauvin has the look of a bandit, and a bandit he is today, having heard the clash of wheels behind him just before Pélussin. It hardly took a split second for the tricolore to accelerate. With him went Gaul, Ockers and Bahamontes, all three after mountains points and all three worried that Gilbert Bauvin might spoil their day.

It was meant to be so simple – climb the two mountains, mop up the points, give up the ghost on the descent and let someone like DeFilippis win. But no. And if Gilbert Bauvin wants the yellow jersey so much, then he's going to have to work for it – their competition is of an entirely different order.

Walkowiak understands what's going through Bauvin's mind right now. The opportunity has presented itself, and he has attacked the Oeillon with everything in his arsenal. He knows that Bauvin can climb, but he doesn't know that Bauvin has gone alone, without teammates. An opportunist he might be, but he's a lone opportunist.

Another rider has left the peloton sensing that his time has come. Jan Adriaenssens, the former yellow jersey, Sterke Jan. Ockers has waited for him, and having brought his teammate into the fold, takes on Bahamontes and Ockers for the mountains points.

The blackboards put Walkowiak at 1'30" back. Deledda has gone, unable to keep up with his teammate's furious pace up the Oeillon. Once more, Walko finds himself alone, unable to take the time to admire the scenery, the chestnut trees and the acacias, unable to feel the welcome relief of the shade from the burning sunlight.

Walkowiak is out of the saddle, pounding at every pedal stroke. Ahead, Bauvin is doing the same, hoping that his pedal strokes are harder, hoping that Walkowiak is weakening. The chase is on, up the Oeillon.

It's a pretty climb, the Oeillon, if you have the time to notice it.

At the peak, Walkowiak has brought the gap down to just 40 seconds. Journalists' pens are out already. This could be something.

Blackboards are being hastily redrawn, and cars are withdrawn as Gilbert Bauvin hits the descent à tombeau ouverte, caring little for his companions who have fought their first battle of the day and who care little for Bauvin and his dreams of yellow. Bauvin takes a full hairpin on them, and then two, his unshaven chin riding into the breeze. Behind, Walkowiak can see his prey down the hill, in between trees, in flashes.

You could argue that the Tour de France is being played out right here, right now, in this moment. Down the Oeillon, something magical is taking place. An opportunist attack is being culled, hairpin by hairpin, by the yellow jersey, despite Bauvin's greatest ever ride.

Bauvin looks up. You should never look up. Look ahead, only look ahead, he tells himself. Stop thinking about the man in pursuit, start thinking about the finish line in Saint-

Etienne. Think of your objective. Forget Walkowiak.

Walkowiak can only think of one thing – getting back to Bauvin, hauling him in. If you thought Walkowiak was incapable of anger, incapable of bring startled from his habitual nonchalance, you are being proven wrong. He can see the gap shrinking in front of his eyes, literally being displayed in front of him as if by magic, cast upon the tarmac: 30 seconds, 29 seconds, 28 seconds. A few more pedal strokes and it's 25. What's that in metres?

And Bauvin has given everything for this escapade. Nothing has been held in reserve, but he has been nervously glancing over his shoulder, anxiously looking up the hill at the man in yellow in hot pursuit, getting ever closer. How is he getting closer? How is he doing this?

The chase effectively ends in Saint-Julien-Molin-Molette, a pretty-sounding village of a few hundred inhabitants, a few of whom have turned out today, gingham tablecloths and vin de table, baguette and cheese, a few French flags here and there. They are unaware of what has just happened, unaware of the pursuit that has just taken place. It has lasted just over 20km, and is a huge moral setback for the tricolore Bauvin who has given his all for this attack only to see a 1'30" lead wiped out in the space of just 20 measly kilometres. How did Walkowiak do it?

And worst of all, the yellow jersey has the cheek to pat him on the back and offer him a bidon full of water, noticing that he's run out. Why does he have to be so nice?

The residents of Saint-Julien-Molin-Molette cheer on the peloton, the cars, the police and the broom wagon, before returning to their newspapers, their idle chat and their lazy afternoon. Bales of hay flutter at the edges as a breeze whips up around the town which quickly returns to normality. The ladies of Saint-Julien-Molin-Molette have all returned indoors, the men have got the cards out. The children are playing Tour de France on the now empty roads – c'est moi Bauvin, et toi t'es Walko.

The Tour has cast its magic upon the town, and left a little dust.

The fact that Stan Ockers won this stage, 4'41" ahead of the yellow jersey group which included Bauvin, Huot and Forestier, is a footnote to this stage. Over the space of those 20km, Roger Walkowiak has written a page in Tour de France history. He could have lost it all, and some may argue later on that he should have lost it all – he would have deserved it – but he fought with every muscle in his body to keep his yellow jersey and risked his life descending the Oeillon.

André Chassaignon is ecstatic. For him, Roger Walkowiak is the latest in a long line of champions, and deserves to win the Tour de France right here, today, in Saint-Etienne.

"To hell with the chronological order! I'll say it now – Roger Walkowiak deserves to win the Tour. I'm still shaking at what I've seen today. I lost my impartiality, I lost my passivity, I lost all professionalism watching this, when I cried 'bravo Roger!' the moment he caught up with Bauvin. I shouldn't do this, I know. A journalist must be objective in all circumstances. But I couldn't help myself. It would have been wrong, it would have been unjust if Walko had been beaten because of this fall. This pursuit on the Oeillon was so poignant, so enthralling, that I say to hell with neutrality – I wanted with all my heart that Walko win. I hope that Bauvin forgives me. If the situation were reversed, I would have wished him the same."

Top Gun And Bidot

Raphaël Géminiani appears to feel the same way. Overheard in conversation with his technical director Marcel Bidot, 'Top Gun' is – as always – open and honest.

"You want to know how I feel? Walko has won the Tour. Don't tell Bauvin. He thought he was in yellow, I can't imagine how he feels."

Bidot is shocked. "Raph, you can't say that. Gilbert is your teammate. If you don't believe he can win, what will become of us? Confidence matters!"

"Look Marcel, I'm a Tour veteran now. I've seen everything. I saw Koblet climbing trees as your brother Jean would have said. I saw Coppi, I never thought I'd see the like of him again. I saw Ferdy Kübler and his "Hop, Ferdi" attacks. I've seen Louison ride through the pain to win even just last year, you remember that don't you. But I'll tell you this, clear as day, Walko is a great champion. What he did there on the Oeillon, that's as good as anything I've ever seen in the Tour. Don't tell me you think otherwise."

"You can't compare Walko to Louison, Gem. Louison's your friend, you admire him so much."

"Why not? That was Louison all over. Losing 1'30" in a crash and chasing them down over 20km. He's won it, and he deserves it."

"But Gilbert is only 3'26" behind, with a time trial to come. And remember, Walko was pushed by Deledda."

"And he got 30 seconds for it. But that changes nothing. Walko did everything else on his own. Everything."

Bidot is appalled. "But you're Gilbert's teammate. You have to help him!"

"Oh, I'll help him. I'll do all I can to help him win, but if you want to know what I'm thinking – it wouldn't be fair. Bauvin failed today. Walko did what he did without his teammates. He won it the right way, fair and square."

Bidot shakes Gem's hand. He knows that 'Top Gun' is a romantic at heart, and he loves adventure. He loves panache. He loves a story.

Déjeuner sur l'herbe, or Walko's Time Trials
26th July 1956
Stage 19, Individual Time Trial from Saint-Etienne to Lyon, 73km

30 Seconds' Sleep

Sauveur knew that his rider had barely slept. He didn't need to look at his pallid, drawn face, or the bloodshot eyes. He'd been asleep half the night listening to Walkowiak tossing and turning, huffing and puffing. And he understood why his rider was worried.

They had tried to keep the news from him, but a loud-mouthed reporter had gatecrashed the team dinner and blubbed all about it. So what about that 30-second penalty, he shouted, how are you going to deal with that? What 30-second penalty? Asked Walkowiak to his teammates. Ah yes, they thought, that 30-second penalty. We were told not to mention it.

They played it down. They even laughed about it.

Ducazeaux knows that none of this is good. In fact, it's very bad. His rider's lead has been reduced by 30 seconds, and he needs every spare second he has if he is going to keep the yellow jersey at the end of this time trial.

"Roger, go back to sleep. It's a time trial so you'll be starting last of all. So I'll come and wake you up at 10, you can do

50km to warm up and then all will be fine. You'll see."

And, miraculously, that's just what Roger does. When Ducazeaux checks in at 8am, Walko is snoring, and even has a smile on his face. Indeed, when Ducazeaux checks in at 10am, he sees Walko fast asleep, turns on his heels and tiptoes back out of the room. Another hour of sleep, he thinks… it won't hurt, will it?

The balance to consider is that Walkowiak needs more time in the saddle to warm up compared to other riders. But Tours are won on good sleep, as Ferdy Kübler always said.

So at midday, Roger Walkowiak finally wakes, eats, gets a massage from his soigneur, and rides 10km. It's not enough. Roger knows it's not enough, Ducazeaux knows it's not enough, but it will have to do.

Time Trials – Not For Everyone

Time trialling is a strange affair, for both audience and riders alike. It suits some men, it doesn't suit others. A rider like Roger Hassenforder, for instance, is not made for two hours on his own. Even on his greatest breakaways, he has someone alongside him just for the conversation, or just to have someone to beat at the finish line. A two-hour ride on his own could bore him into a stupor.

Today's time trial is a 73km, up-and-down affair that starts in the Stade Geoffroy-Guitard, an ash velodrome that requires skill to navigate. There are some Breton boys who just want to do loops of the velodrome. Forget the time trial.

The riders start alongside the stop-clock, take a full tour of the velodrome, before exiting and finding themselves encouraged by crowds of people lining the streets of the Saint-Etienne suburbs. Quickly, those crowds dissipate as the rider passes a filling station, and a few curves later, he is out in the middle of nowhere. On his own, save the team car and, if he's of any importance, a motorbike.

For the spectator, the time trial offers – on the one hand – the opportunity to see every rider up close, at approximately three-minute gaps. A full day's entertainment, free of charge. On the other hand, the tension and the excitement is all playing out on paper. Time gaps are almost impossible to call when you're stood on a hill eating your sandwich, but those with a radio will be able to follow the action more closely.

To all intents and purposes, the day's action goes like this:

1. Cyclist approaches
2. Note down the name written on the front of the car following him
3. Encourage the cyclist by name
4. Wait a couple of minutes
5. Another cyclist approaches
6. Repeat

The better riders will come later, of course. So it would pay not to wear yourself out over the likes of Chaussabel, lanterne rouge, and first man past the first checkpoint, if you can call it a checkpoint.

Bienvenue au But

The But d'Arpin is perhaps the best place to be a spectator, if you can find a spot. There, you'll find mobile ice cream salesmen moving through the picnickers, sausage stalls (we are approaching Lyon, after all), sandwich sellers. You'll find the litter from the caravane publicitaire, which passed through over an hour before Chaussabel kicked things off. The irony is that the lanterne rouge received perhaps his biggest cheer of the entire Tour. Something of a highlight for Chaussabel, but even he acknowledged that the excessive amounts of vin de table being consumed may have played a role.

It was close to the But d'Arpin that Malléjac, whose Tour has mostly taken place in anonymity, overtook Nolten the Dutchman and received a roar of approval, and a few turned heads from the bored children who had seen a few cyclists already and were beginning to wonder what all the fuss was about.

There's a Spaniard, shouts one eager father to his picnicking family. He's not meant to be here now. Oi, Diego, he shouts, que pasa? He laughs. A funny joke.

But it's not funny for Miguel Bover, who has overtaken two already. Miguel Bover has spent this Tour attempting to serve Federico Bahamontes, but has fallen out of the peloton more times than can be counted. But Miguel loves a time trial, and he has already overtaken Camille Huyghe, he of Nord-est-Centre fame as well as Kemp from the Luxembourg team. Bover is steaming up the But d'Arpin with all the regularity of a locomotive, legs like pistons, eyes boring into the far distance. Bover is on his way to overtake seven more riders and post what is set to be one of the best times of the day.

By mid-afternoon, every rider is out on the road, and that includes the two men most likely to win this Tour: Bauvin and Walkowiak. But there are rumours going around that Jan Adriaensens, Sterke Jan, is flying. Someone has a radio, and is shouting out time gaps to the picnicking crowd, some of whom are showing an interest. And here he is, sooner than he should have been.

Sterke Jan also quite likes a time trial. Who knew? The radio puts him at just a few seconds behind Bover, who has already posted 1:46:57. Sylvère Maes, Belgian Team Director, is standing upright through the sunroof of the 203, hollering encouragement. "You're just seconds behind, Jan. Stay strong, stay sterke. You can do it, boy, you can do it!"

The assembled crowds know that beyond Adriaanssens, there are only a handful of riders to go, and that includes Walko.

Bauvin rides through with minimal effort, dancing on his pedals and stopwatches are set. Where is Walko? It'll be three minutes at most, someone shouts. Any more and he's losing time. It's eerily silent on the hill as parents send their children down as scouts. Wave when you see him.

The three minutes is up already – that's the gap between the riders when they set off. A noise at the bottom alerts those at the top that Walko is on his way. There's a crescendo of sound and encouragement all the way up the climb, which is stiff and stiffer than it should be for our yellow jersey. Already, Walko is a full 30 seconds behind as he hits the climb of the But d'Arpin, and a full minute behind as he reaches the top. He's losing time – some say he's losing the yellow jersey.

He doesn't look right, he doesn't look easy. Is he really going to win the Tour like this? Allez Walko, Allez. You'll make it. Allez.

And with Walko gone, the police follow. More team cars, beeping their horns. Some of the police wave at the children, which makes their day. Picnics are wrapped up in their blankets and dropped unceremoniously back into baskets. Children are relieved that their ordeal is over and, not so secretly, so are the wives. The men are wondering about Walko.

Wondering About Walko

They're right to wonder. It's a struggle, and Walko is fighting to maintain any kind of regularity in his pedalling. He's shifting from one side of the road to the other, even as the But d'Arpin levels out. Ducazeaux is shouting from behind, stay focused, stay in line. Remember everything I told you.

It is doubtful Roger can hear.

In Lyon, Jan Adriaenssens has crossed the line just one second slower than the Spaniard Bover. He doesn't care, because he has realised what this means. He's closer to Bauvin, and even closer to Roger Walkowiak than he had hoped to be at the start of the day. The baker boy has hopes.

When Roger Walkowiak crosses the line, he is two minutes down on Gilbert Bauvin, and his GC lead is cut to a miserable 85 seconds.

1'25" is all he has with two stages left to ride.

As he slumps to the railings, he looks back on a bad day. The last few kilometres were the worst, he thinks. The worst he's ridden over the last 3 weeks. A succession of potholes he should have missed, a flurry of bends he could have taken better, if he'd been focused enough. But even if he'd got it right, even if he'd done it perfectly, it was all too late. The time had been lost long ago, back on the But d'Arpin in front of all of those fans Walko wanted to impress. Cast aside your doubts, he wanted to say, Walko is here.

When the crowds of the But d'Arpin got home that evening, the mood in the Walkowiak camp had turned from disappointment into a strange form of resilience. It's funny how a team's morale can switch, perhaps with a few choice words from Ducazeaux, perhaps with a few barbed comments from rival teams. We've still got this, they say. We've still got the Tour in our hands. Two flat stages, one ceremonial… all Roger has to do is stay on his bike and hold off the attacks, and when he reaches the next finish town, he'll have won the Tour.

Did anyone mention that the next finish town is Roger Walkowiak's home town of Montluçon?

Leave Me Here in Montluçon, My Dear
27th July 1956
Stage 21, Lyon to Montluçon, 237km

The Heat and the Cold

It is hot. It has been hot for weeks now, at least in these parts. A Tour that started under grey skies in Reims has mostly baked under a scorching sun, and is now showing signs. Tan lines are more defined. Riders are participating in the traditional chasse à la canette – the chase for the can of sugared beer. It helps on these long, hot, flat stages.

The heat didn't help Walko sleep last night. Sauveur Ducazeaux had kept his windows closed during the day to keep the hot air out, and he'd have even sung his rider a lullaby if he could. It wasn't really the heat that had got to Walko, it was the pressure. 1'25" could be wiped out in the flattening of an inner tube. After all this work, after all this confidence...

The heat doesn't help Charly Gaul, either. While most riders turn southwards for their strength, Gaul turns skywards. The cooler the better, and his late surge in the Alps has seen him climb the mountains classification which – realistically – was his only aim in this Tour. A climb over a relative molehill early on in this stage outside Lyon would see him clinch the title ahead of poor Valentin Huot whose dominance earlier on in the race – at least over mountains – faded somewhat as Gaul discovered the Alpine cool, and – of course – Italy.

His victory was met with a smattering of unwitting applause. Did anyone realise? Did anyone actually care? Even Charly Gaul might admit that he didn't.

The real question of the day was, of course, whether Gilbert Bauvin or Jan Adriaenssens would attack. Bauvin would require the support of the French team, of course. Adriaenssens would naturally rely on a strong Belgian team. Walko only had Adolphe Deledda.

One Last Crazy Escapade

Surveying the situation was none other than Roger Hassenforder. Hassen felt good. Hassen felt confident. He looked round and saw the yellow jersey safely in the wheel of Bauvin. He saw Adriaenssens head down, applying little effort. The riders had looked each other in the whites of the eyes, and had decided not to attack, not to ride.

It's my day, declared Hassenforder, before leaping from the peloton with over 180km to go. A few heads bobbed up. One or two may have noticed that Hassen had tied a small doll to the back of his saddle. A lucky charm, Hassen would say.

20km into his escape, Hassen receives the visit of André Leducq in the Miroir des Sports car.

"What are you riding today Roger?"

"54 x 14 André. That'll hurt them, won't it!" beamed Hassenforder.

Leducq looked impressed. "You're telling me. That's what we'd use to ride behind motorbikes in my day. Keep it up, boy. Keep it up."

Leducq winds his head in and turns to Chassaignon. "He's

riding a 54 x 14, the fool. He'll never last like that."

"André, it's something to write about. We need him."

50km into Hassenforder's breakaway, he receives a visit from Tour director Félix Lévitan himself. It's clearly serious.

"Will I win if I carry on like this?" asks the Alsacien.

"Why of course you will, my boy. And you'll get the combativity prize again. You're over 4 minutes up on the peloton. They're all dozing."

With 35km to go, Lévitan pulls up alongside once more.

"Come on, Roger. I can see you're flagging. Don't give in now."

Hassenforder can barely bring himself to look up from his handlebars. "I'm cooked, Félix. Cooked."

"Rubbish, boy. You've got barely an hour's riding to go."

With 20km to go, cars are overtaking him, but Lévitan makes sure to inform his man that he has 14 minutes on the next rider. Hassenforder takes his doll in his hands, clenches it and finds something extra as the false flat that has been sapping his energy turns into the false descent, and Montluçon appears on the horizon, imperceptible at first, but a collection of church spires and somewhere along that road, the velodrome where this 180km breakaway would end.

Les Dames Walkowiak

In this velodrome, two women sit side-by-side. One, younger, wears a light pink dress and sits behind a display of dark pink roses, and a sign that proclaims "La Rose Walkowiak". One could argue that she is the Walko Rose herself, but a local horticulturalist has created the flower especially for her husband, Roger Walkowiak. Or, he created the flower and has now found a name for it, because not even the most clairvoyant of horticulturalists would have known that Roger

Walkowiak would soon become the winner of the Tour de France.

The way Pierrette is shifting in her seat, you could argue that not even Pierrette is confident her husband would soon become the winner of the Tour de France.

From her position, she can see the gap between the stands in the velodrome, and between that gap, she can see the bridge over the river Cher.

Pierrette turns to the lady next to her. "Did you see that?" She points. "A rider has just crossed the bridge. Look."

The lady in grey crosses and uncrosses her hands. Wipes the sweat from her palms. She is Roger Walkowiak's mother. She has the look of a Walkowiak: round cheeks, small eyes, kindly. Only this Walkowiak has stuck to the diet of lard, beef and carrot, fried potatoes, andouillette. She envies the hold Pierrette has over her son's diet, but if pushed, would grudgingly accept that she has been a good influence on her boy.

What both women share is a belief that this was Roger's destiny. Unlike most people here in Montluçon, or indeed around France itself, they have both always believed that Roger had what it takes to win a major race. Perhaps it's blind faith, but perhaps they knew something. Only they were watching him in the Dauphiné while others were watching Louison. Only they read about his stage win in the Vuelta last year. Only they connected the dots.

Mother Walkowiak nudges her daughter-in-law. The man who crossed the bridge, he's coming into the velodrome now. White jersey, red hoop.

What the Walkowiak women don't notice is that Roger Hassenforder has emptied himself of all his resources. He has nothing left but adrenaline. He's heaving himself around the bends, desperate to stay upright and not embarrass himself.

He feels the salty tears fall from his eyes. Of all the breakaways, of all the lone, madcap escapades Roger Hassenforder has attempted, this is the craziest, the maddest, the finest.

"He's called Roger," shouts Pierrette, excited. "That's a good sign, isn't it?"

The old lady isn't convinced. Yet.

The Hassenforder Roger collapses into the arms of Leon Le Calvez, his technical director, and at a distance, he is just another tired cyclist forced to the extremities of his abilities for our entertainment. A small man in the distance who has won a stage of a bike race. Eyes are mostly now focused on the bridge in the gap between buildings.

Rumours have gone round. Walko has fallen. Walko is fine. Bauvin has attacked. Bauvin has not attacked. Adriaenssens is in a breakaway. There is no breakaway. How would anyone know? It feels like an age since the Hassenforder Roger came into the velodrome. Look at him now, he's laid out on the grass, he's even joking around. It's been five minutes.

Another lone cyclist has gone over the bridge. He's not wearing a yellow jersey. It looks like a red one. A Spaniard.

He is welcomed into the velodrome with warmth and appreciation, if not fervour. He's not our boy.

And time still expands in front of our eyes. Every second is observed.

And then, in the distance, a barely perceptible roar. It grows, quickly, like a virus spreading from person to person, exponentially. And from the side of a building, over the bridge over the river Cher, a whole peloton of Tour de France competitors, and safely among them is one man in a yellow jersey.

"Walko!" shout the crowd, almost as one, but not quite. "He's there! He's coming home!"

The ladies Walkowiak have to rise, not because their view

is obstructed, but because it feels the right thing to do, given that everyone else has done. There is a clapping of boards, a waving of hands, a demonstration of pride that their home town boy, Roger Walkowiak, has come good at the ripe age of 29.

The townsfolk had spent the morning decking the town of Montluçon out in yellow. Yellow drapes. Any yellow flowers they could harvest. Yellow ribbons. The townspeople are wearing any yellow clothes they can find. It is this display that welcomes Walko. He had promised himself no tears, but he can't stop them from falling as he enters the roads he knows so well. Training rides through town and out into country, back through town and into the hills. He knows every turn, every pothole, every cobblestone. He knows to avoid the slight camber. He knows the angle to approach the velodrome. But he doesn't know Montluçon like this. So many people. So much love.

Leave Me Here in Montluçon

There are signs hanging from balconies. We love Walko. Allez Walko. He is a rider transformed, not just in performance, but in name. The transformation is complete, he is no longer Walkowiak, but Walko – shortened and adored in equal measure. The same number of letters as Bobet and Coppi, he thinks, as he looks up at one banner which has the 'O' of Walko turned into a heart. And yet still he doubts. And he doubts all the way to the finish line, two banks around the velodrome. He doubts they've come for him, despite the clamour and the noise. Surely not. This can't be happening.

And it is. Towns like Montluçon need moments like this. Local heroes in moments of serendipity – bringing the yellow jersey to the town of his birth and his childhood, the town in which he worked as a metalworker for so many years, the town in which he married. Few would admit that the name Walkowiak meant anything to them before this Tour, but few would begrudge Walko his moment, because his moment is their moment. A Montluçien explosion of civic pride.

The Walkowiak Roger has left his bike, and has found the Hassenforder Roger. Both men are crying, and fall into each others' arms. What are we doing? they ask each other. What is going on?

"How long have you been here?" asks the Walkowiak Roger.

"I don't know, but I think I've grown a beard since I arrived," jokes the Hassenforder Roger.

"You're nuts," adds the Walkowiak Roger, to which the Hassenforder Roger just nods and laughs. "But your team – please thank them from me. They stopped every attack today trying to protect your escape."

And this last bit is a little-known fact about the penultimate stage of the 1956 Tour de France. That the Breton team, in trying to protect their man, effectively neutralised the peloton, protecting the Walkowiak Roger as well as the Hassenforder Roger. A French team too disinterested in helping Gilbert Bauvin had a go – but found themselves marked. The Belgians gave up quickly, with Adriaenssens seemingly happy with a place on the podium.

Next, the Walkowiak Roger enters the stands, finding his way through the barriers, and embraces wife then mother. The correct order, he thinks to himself. He spots the roses on his way past and thinks to himself, this really is happening. They've named a rose after me.

Sauveur Ducazeaux has missed much of the party. The team cars had been held up, but the yellow jersey did at least mean that the Nord-Est-Centre car was well-positioned in the peloton des bagnoles that had to re-form some miles outside of Montluçon, as is the tradition.

He would allow his rider some adulation. After all, this is his patch and these are his people. But is the yellow jersey really his?

Bauvin and Adriaenssens failed to attack today, but he remembers Robic and the Tour won 100km from Paris. He knows how this Tour has been ridden in bursts of personal ambition and knows that neither man will allow Walkowiak to be crowned the winner one night before they reach Paris. There is still distance to be covered.

Sauveur Ducazeaux's Long Night In

There is a crowd of clamouring admirers outside the team hotel. Sauveur Ducazeaux has taken on a new role tonight, that of doorman. Visitors keep on coming.

"But sir, I'm a childhood friend of Walko, I have to see him."

"Yeah, and I'm Grace Kelly. Go away," shouts Ducazeaux.

"When he finds out, he'll be furious with you," shouts the childhood friend. "You'll see!"

"You can talk to him after the Tour. He's asleep now, and absolutely nobody shall disturb him, do you understand?"

Another upstart wants to shake Roger's hand.

"And you – out of here. No one is going down this corridor."

"But we went to school together, he'll understand."

"Yes, yes, he'll understand very well when you come and shake his hand after he's got back from Paris. Now scoot."

Ducazeaux wonders aloud – why, oh why, this year of all years, did they have to end the penultimate stage in Montluçon? There are 2,000 people outside waving flags and chanting Walko's name. Why, I'd bet at least half of them had never heard of him until yesterday.

Ducazeaux has been wily, however. He has draped the

yellow jersey over the balcony of what was Roger Walkowiak's bedroom which looks out over the main square, where the crowds are gathered. Roger himself is sleeping in Ducazeaux's room, towards the back of the hotel.

He has positioned Adolphe Deledda in the foyer of the hotel to catch any rogue 'childhood friends' of Roger's, with the instructions that he is to tell any intruder that Roger and Sauveur have driven to Néris-les-Bains by car.

"But he said he'd meet me here," one pleads. "He's waiting for me."

"Ah," nods Deledda. "He'll have forgotten."

Sauveur Ducazeaux tiptoes into his own bedroom to spy on his rider. Realising he's fast asleep, Ducazeaux tiptoes back out, ruffles around in his pockets for those earplugs he bought from the pharmacy earlier, and heads to Walko's room for, perhaps, a few hours' sleep.

Les Ivrognes

As the crowds thin out, discussions turn to tomorrow and whether Walko can hold on. There's talk about finding the French team's hotel and keeping Bauvin awake all night, but loyalty to Darrigade and Géminiani forbids this. The songs and the ribaldry carry on long into the night in the bars and clubs of Montluçon. The restaurants have given away more bottles of wine than they would have sold in a week, and the agneau bourbonnais has been flying out of the kitchens since early evening.

Gaston Bénac has enjoyed a local pudding as part of his café gourmande, perhaps his twentieth such pudding, notes Chassaignon. Three weeks on the road with Gaston is enough to turn a man into a vegetarian hermit, he muses, but he knows that within two hours of returning to Paris, he'll be itching for the road again. Itching for moments like this evening in Montluçon, and tonight has an end-of-holiday feel for the journalists. How marvellous, he acknowledges, that we landed here in this delightful town, in this delightful restaurant, with this delightful yellow jersey.

"Such serendipity", muses Bénac, not for the first time. Chassaignon watches his colleague attack the Café Gourmande. Three small puddings and a coffee.

"Such wonderful serendipity," he insists. "Ah, André, I've seen Tours come and I've seen Tours go, I've seen the Maes brothers, I've seen Speicher, I've seen Coppi, but never have we landed in the birth town of the winning rider the night before Paris."

Chassaignon runs through the previous winners in his head, noting that it would have been geographically impossible. Coppi and Bartali, forget it. Bobet, Robic, both in Brittany – forget it. Koblet and Kübler, both in Switzerland, forget it. Perhaps if Anquetil were to win a Tour when he's older. Rouen, isn't it? He's lost in thoughts.

Serendipity, he agrees. Indeed. There are precious few people in the restaurant now, most have stumbled home.

A little digestif, perhaps, Bénac wonders instructively to the waiter who just happened to be passing, who now nods appreciatively. Chassaignon makes the sign that there will be two digestifs, and the night carries on a little longer.

The bands have played their last, and the revelry is played out to a backdrop of drunken songs outside, edging gradually into the distance. Slowly, the fountains disgorge themselves of drunken revellers, the sound of songs echoing in the distance as the sound of fountain water hitting ground returns, alone once more. And back home, alone too, Pierrette in pink dreams of Paris, and finally being reunited with her husband.

Montluçon falls silent.

Take Me Back to Montluçon
28th July 1956
Stage 22, Montluçon to Paris, 331km

Lunch In The Heart of France (Almost)

Bruère-Allichamps lies at the very heart of France. Its geographical centre. Like many towns of the region, it is a drive-through town. A place you stop if you're unfortunate enough to run out of petrol, or if you've made the wrong decision.

For André Chassaignon, Miroir des Sports journalist, it is a place of pilgrimage.

André Leducq, former Tour winner tourned journalist, is not happy.

"André, give up, will you? The peloton is too close. We'll never find anywhere to eat round here."

"If we get ahead of them... take the back roads, put your foot down."

"No, we'll find somewhere nearby for lunch."

Chassaignon huffs. He had visions of himself, propping up the bar at the geographical heart of his country, with a fresh glass of white, the glass speckled with condensation. He'd raise the glass to la France, reflect on the Tour that is coming to its close. Chassaignon is a romantic.

He is stuck with Leducq and Bénac in a bistro 2km north of his country's heart. The Tour doesn't pass by here. It doesn't even so much as touch upon it. There are no cycling posters, there is no cycling chit-chat. There are no bikes outside. The men are unrecognised. To improve this pitiful situation, the former Tour de France winner André Leducq tears into Roger Walkowiak's teammates.

"Not good enough, none of them. They wouldn't get into my team, I tell you."

"Do go on," mumbles Bénac as he gorges himself on the free baguette.

"Have you seen them at all since we left Reims? Hm?"

Chassaignon admits he had, once or twice. But the point has been made.

"They left Reims with modest ambitions," he continues, "and modest careers if we're to be fully honest with ourselves. Not one of them wanted anything other than to reach Paris, take some bonus money here and there, and go home.

"Now, one of them – I won't say who – but we all know the man I'm talking about, he's used to abandoning when it gets too hard. But with Walko earning him a fortune, he's spent half the Tour lolling around at the back of the peloton drinking sugared beer. But look at them today, just like yesterday, they're at the front of the peloton, proving that it's just as easy to ride at the front sucking up the dust for the other riders as it is to ride at the back drinking beer and fetching water.

"It's a question of attitude. That's all it is. Attitude. If they wanted to do this for themselves, they'd have done it – but they haven't had the attitude until now. Why is that? They're lazy, that's why."

Bénac has run out of baguette, and has run out of patience with Leducq.

"You've lost your romanticism, Leducq."

"Fiddlesticks!" he exclaims, visibly offended. "I'm as romantic as they get!"

"Don't talk shit. You rode the Tour. You know the difference between the men at the front and the men at the back. They're worth just as much in any Tour, they write our words for us. They're the best men from their towns and they're part of the colour, the scenery of the Tour. Leave them alone."

"They could have done this all along, that's all I'm saying!"

"Phooey! Ah…", he breaks off. "Here's the food."

The three munch happily, in the knowledge that the breakaway has called off its skirmishes and that Roger Walkowiak is riding to victory in Paris without much of a fuss. Chassaignon writes up notes from the morning.

Darrigade attacked first. Bauvin followed. Walkowiak took to his wheel with Scribante his teammate. Some Belgians – who were they – Impanis, Adriaenssens too of course, Deledda was in there wasn't he? Yes, old Adolphe, he would have to be up there.

"How many did you count, Gaston?"

Mouth full of chicken leg. "Mmf, twenty or so?"

Twenty Men

Bénac was right. Twenty riders took the initiative, 331km away from Paris, to break away from the dozing peloton and ride hard. 50km per hour, some men bent over their handlebars, attacking each other and more importantly, attacking Roger Walkowiak. Darrigade, offering a neat coda to a Tour that he so effortlessly tore apart upon its departure from Reims, was either leading out Gilbert Bauvin for an attack, or he was hoping for more personal glory. A repeat of Reims, perhaps. It was too soon for that.

The rain had started falling, the road was slippy, the wind had risen. After 20km of trying to kill each other with bicycles, the leading men called off the attack. Let's just ride. Roger's won.

And so they ride through the anonymous fields of central France. Straight roads, bursts of rain, like a family returning from holiday. The way south, everything holds promise. The weather improves with each kilometre, hopes rise. The way north, the hope fades, the light disappears, the clouds mass. Let's just get home, unpack the bags, put the washing on. Finish this thing.

When you're returning from holiday, passing attractions are wilfully ignored. Fun for somebody else, perhaps, emptied of holidaymakers. The riders are unaware that the Foire aux Sorcières takes place in one of these villages they pass through. They say that such a festival has taken place here since Medieval times. Locals dress as witches and shamans, they beat drums, they boil vegetables in a cauldron and drink soup the colour of blood (beetroot, of course), and dance until moon-down.

They are perhaps also unaware of the castle at Sully-sur-Loire and the Saint-Benoit Abbey. If the Tour is a pilgrimage, it is apt, perhaps, that it should pass by one of France's most sacred lieux de pélerinage.

The Tour is breathing its last. Adriaenssens has a last-gasp attempt at glory around Etampes, but it's embarrassing. Walkowiak hovers behind on his wheel and gives him a look as if to say "why?". Bauvin has punctured – perhaps it was a claim for second place – but Bergaud has given him his wheel and the encyclopaedia salesman is back in the group.

A small group breaks away, but no one really important is in it, and they are left to compete for the day's prizes while the real prize awaits. Nencini takes the stage by a nose length ahead of Desmet, Le Ber and Mirando, and the Parc des Princes falls silent as it awaits the yellow jersey.

A Warm Welcome For Walko

Now, there are those who might say that Roger Walkowiak was booed on his entrance into the Parc des Princes velodrome, and they would be wrong. The reception he received was warm, if not adulatory. This is the yellow jersey, after all. He has been transformed from the humble nobody Walkowiak to the five-lettered superstar Walko, and there are those who stand for Walko, there are those who shout his name, but this is not Montluçon. It is muted in comparison.

The boos, they were reserved for Marcel Bidot. The Parisians expected better. They expected Louison Bobet, and if not Louison then they expected Géminiani. Surely it was his turn? Or Bauvin, for Christ's sake, anyone in a French shirt. In Paris, they don't do regional teams, even if they do have an Ile-de-France team lost somewhere in that peloton.

Bidot deserved his boos, they say, he let us all down. He let a regional rider win.

For Walko, then, the spoils. He is carried by the crowd and his teammates, he is showered with flowers. He is, somehow, underwhelmed. They aren't celebrating me, not like my friends in Montluçon, he thinks. They're celebrating the yellow jersey. The ritual of the Tour. And it's fine to be a part of that, he thinks. Everything is fine. But it's not what he thought it might be. They didn't want me, they wanted someone else – anyone else. They wanted a tricolore or a grande champion like Bobet, Coppi, Koblet, Kübler. Not a metalworker from Montluçon.

And so, in anticlimax, ends what may be one of the finest and most competitive Tours ever ridden. Few other than

Felix Goddet and a handful of journalists will recognise this. The French public wanted a hero in the mould of Bobet, and instead they found an unassuming 29-year-old from the countryside, a man who would rather go fishing or spend time with his wife Pierrette than celebrate at the casino or the restaurant. A man whose name they could barely pronounce. A man they had never heard of.

Over the last three weeks, the fans have seen multiple yellow jerseys. They've seen racing as fast as the Tour has ever seen. They've witnessed Charly Gaul at his majestic best – and his woeful worst. They've seen the mother of all breakaways on the road to Angers, and they've seen the renaissance of Roger Hassenforder – four stages, all of them magnificent in their own crazy way.

And they've seen Roger Walkowiak. And some who hold a longer view of the sport have hopes that Walko is the new Bobet. However, a decade of golden era heroics has ill-prepared the cycling fan for this technical, athletic Tour. Some wonder if this is the future. Will it always be like this? A Tour winner who doesn't win stages, who seeks a mathematical advantage by quietly slipping into the right breaks and staying consistent?

Few would realise that they had seen one of the Tour's legends. Many thought that this would pass. A new hero would come next year. Young Anquetil, perhaps. Or that Bobet would return, fitter than ever. This is temporary.

Roger says to himself: Everything is fine. He looks at the sour faces of the Parisians and he feels that despite their applause, they resent him. He's not one of them, and he never will be.

Take me back to Montluçon, Pierrette. To my fishing rod and my hearth. To my people. To my local criteriums and my agneau bourbonnais. Take me back to the wooden buildings and the wide, open spaces, to the rolling hills and the long evenings spent riding with friends as the blood-orange sun fails to drop below the skyline, to the quiet of my Montluçon. Take this yellow jersey off me, take me back to the anonymous man I was. Take me home.

Everything is fine. Everything will be fine.

Final Thoughts - Epilogue

Be There Every Day

An immediate analysis of this Tour de France would underline Antonin Magne's theory that you don't win the Tour unless you're involved every day.

Gaul, Bahamontes, Ockers and Brankart had left Reims believing that they would be competing for the yellow jersey in the mountains, but did any of them believe that they'd be so far behind by the time the Tour reached the Pyrenees? Losing ten minutes one day could be considered a mistake, but to lose ten minutes every day is foolish.

Remember, these men – Gaul, winner of the Giro d'Italia. Ockers – world champion. Brankart – 2nd in the previous Tour. Bahamontes, the Eagle of Toledo, one of the world's finest climbers. These were not régionales.

Jan Adriaenssens may be the rider who came closest, despite finishing behind Gilbert Bauvin. But for some 'bad fish' (we all know it was drugs), Sterke Jan could have won this Tour, and perhaps by a handsome distance. That day, he lost 8 minutes to Walkowiak, and clawed back five of those minutes subsequently to finish just three back.

But to focus on the errors of others, or the lack of previous Tour winners, would be to discredit Roger Walkowiak's victory. Find a Tour winner who hasn't benefited from the errors of others. Indeed, find any sporting hero who hasn't taken advantage of his opponents' misfortunes at some point. The Tour, even in its heroic era, was about consistency. Be there every day, stick to your plan, and your chance will come.

Sauveur Ducazeaux would take credit, and indeed he would welcome credit for having helped Walko win the Tour. Does this devalue Walko's victory in any way? To Walkowiak, it did. As the Tour settled in the memory, Ducazeaux began to embellish here and exaggerate there. Just a little, but enough to rub Walkowiak up the wrong way. It was almost as if Walkowiak were Ducazeaux's toy cyclist, riding entirely at the whim of a master strategist who was moving his armies on the battlefield.

The initial response to Walko's win was one of elation among the journalistic community. Antoine Blondin had previously written witheringly in L'Equipe that Walkowiak was a poujadiste egaré dans le bottin mondain, a country boy lost in the city (among other available translations). He was the first to change his tune. And, indeed, he apologised as he recognised that cycling itself was undergoing a significant transformation. More athletic, more technical, cycling has evolved from a sport of pure talent to a sport of hard work. "Walkowiak embodied this more than anyone, showing courage and consistency."

Jacques Goddet was rapturous, waxing lyrical about the democratisation of cycling and the élargissement du droit à l'accession – the widening of the right of succession. Walkowiak was not a bargain-bin winner – this was a man who has blossomed at precisely the right time.

Louison Bobet was the first to warn Walkowiak of what was

to come, however.

"The hard part starts now. The second win is always the toughest – if it comes at all. The esteem in which one rider holds another who has followed the same path only grows. I would love to help him avoid the pitfalls of victory, those that I have myself had to circumvent and navigate my way through. I was like you, Roger, in 1948. I had never won the Tour but I had known, for the first time, what popularity could do to a man. It places demands upon you, and once popularity has its grip on you, it won't let go. You'll be tempted by what's on offer. I suffered that year, I suffered terribly. But you have more experience than I had then. But watch yourself now, a new life has begun, a life strewn with obstacles and hurdles. Don't make the same mistakes I made."

Louison Bobet

Others would go as far as to suggest that Walkowiak's victory was that of a sniper. Hidden from view, Walkowiak could win the Tour, but in uniform? Without the benefit of surprise, could Walko repeat 1956?

The manner in which Walko became Walkowiak again is worth telling…

Dousset and Piel

Cycling in 1956 was managed by two men. Daniel Dousset and Roger Piel. These two former riders claimed the majority of post-Tour criteriums for themselves. When a town decides to hold a criterium, they call either Dousset or Piel to organise it. The riders give the organiser 10% of their earnings, which make up more than enough to get them through the winter and into the early spring training.

Dousset had been around longer than Piel. Their rivalry began in 1954 when Piel quit cycling and went into competition with Dousset. But Dousset had the champions. The little black book.

In 1955, Walkowiak made a decision that a fair few other cyclists made, given that his former teammate Piel was popular among the riders and was offering better terms. He jumped from Dousset to Piel. After all, if Dousset has all the stars, what chance do I have, wondered Walkowiak.

A year later, as the Tour entered La Rochelle, Dousset turns up in person and meets the organisers of the La Rochelle post-tour criterium. "We'd like the stars of this Tour," they declared, "and if Walkowiak wins the Tour overall, then we'll double – no, triple – his fee."

Dousset is delighted. Walko signs.

Walkowiak is worried that Piel will find out about his criterium contract, and had also neglected to inform Dousset of his arrangement with Piel.

On writing to Piel, Walkowiak is clearly embarrassed, but decides to break off his contract with Piel, who writes back warning him that he is acting against his own interests.

Dousset remained unaware of the on-off relationship, but cared little for Walkowiak. The organisers at La Rochelle – and indeed, organisers around the country – could hold their criteriums without Walkowiak. After all, he didn't come with a huge value attached. There would be Bobet, Géminiani and the tricolores. Who wants a regional rider? He got lucky anyway, didn't he?

Time, and journalists, had tainted the yellow jersey – we'll have Ockers instead.

So Roger Walkowiak didn't win a single post-Tour criterium, nor did he win as much money as, say, a Bobet or a Coppi. He was beginning to find out that life as a Tour winner was tough, as Louison predicted.

So poor Roger Walkowiak went back to Montluçon without the promised riches, and without a manager. To make a bad situation worse, his beloved locals falsely believed that he was living the high life. "He's making 400,000 francs a race," they would say, "he's bought a new car, just look at him, he's not our Walkowiak any more," all of which is unfortunate. Not even Louison earned 400,000 francs a race, and Roger's new car was a simple 403, which he bought to replace the 203.

Hugo Koblet would have grimaced at the thought of a 403.

Revisionist History

The 1957 Tour saw Roger Walkowiak integrated into the French team for the first time in France. It also saw the first appearance in a Grand Tour for the young starlet Jacques Anquetil. Once more André Darrigade won the first stage, and the first yellow jersey, and throughout the first few stages, Roger Walkowiak found himself at the front once more.

He was even starting to assume the position of an experienced old hand. On the stage into Rouen, Jacques Anquetil was desperate to win in front of his home crowd. So desperate, in fact, that he took more turns on the front than was healthy, and nearly broke himself while Bahamontes took a free ride on his wheel. The 1956 champion put his arm around the youngster and gave him some friendly advice that he should save his energy and let riders like Bahamontes do some work, too.

As the Tour reached Flanders, Roger Walkowiak found himself in a group of 13 riders including Anquetil and Bauvin. They had climbed the Muur van Geraardsbergen and crested the Kapelmuur at which point, mathematically, Roger Walkowiak became the virtual yellow jersey on the road with the current leader having suffered a fall. Could it all be happening again?

Unfortunately not. A fall 7km from the finish saw Walkowiak without a wheel, and without help. Of all people, it was Sauveur Ducazeaux, still Technical Director of the Nord-Est-Centre team, who handed the unlucky Walkowiak a wheel. That day, Walkowiak lost 5 minutes on Bauvin, but was praised for his calm, his sang-froid.

Health problems arose as Walkowiak tumbled down the general classification. Bronchitis didn't stop him from riding, but as the Tour reached the Pyrenees, Walkowiak felt the old form returning. He attacked over the col de Port and on the Portet d'Aspet and finished in the leading bunch. Was Walko back?

Alas, no. The French team was struck by a stomach bug. No drugs this time, the riders had been subjected to severe changes in temperature, from blistering heat to a glacial cold on the descent of the Puymorens. A bug brought over from North Africa had started to spread among the team, and was worsened by the sudden climactic changes. Of those to suffer, Walkowiak suffered the most. Unable to sleep, vomiting all night, Walko pulled out of the Tour and was never the same.

Almost immediately – and without shame – the French press went to work. "He clearly didn't deserve to win the 1956 Tour," they wrote.

Roger went from Walko to Walkowiak. And his Tour went from a glorious victory to the now-fabled Tour à la Walkowiak – a derogatory term for a Tour that was won by chance. A casual insult born from the short memories of revisionist historians. Over time, the insult has morphed a little. Any victory à la Walkowiak is unexpected at best, unwarranted at worst. It's an insult to the Roger Walkowiak of 1956 who fought every day to be in the right moves, to hold on to his yellow jersey or to win back yellow. To the Roger Walkowiak who fought for his yellow jersey on the Oeillon, who slid quietly into the breakaway to Angers and who climbed the Croix de Fer.

Roger Walkowiak would always refuse to discuss the 1956 Tour, tainted as it was by the words of those journalists in 1957 who refused to believe he should have won the year before.

They murdered the yellow jersey, he would say.

And that's it.

And so ends my own revisionist history. I have spent months poring over old editions of newspapers, of biographies of the likes of Darrigade, Hassenforder and of course Walko himself. I have irritated my wife by scattering old Miroir des Sports around the living room, and leaving my cycling books in various nooks and crannies around the house.

I chose, because of the COVID-19 lockdown, to publish this ahead of time as a blog, a stage a day, and this encouraged me to look afresh at a book that I had mostly written over Christmas last year. Walko (the book) is more a collection of short stories from the same Tour than an actual book, and that kind of fits. A Tour is a tapestry of tales woven together against the backdrop of the French countryside, its towns and villages coming together in the heat of summer. And that's what I wanted to portray, almost as much as I wanted to emphasise the value of Roger Walkowiak's victory.

The more I read about the achievements of riders such as Hassenforder, Darrigade, Caput and the like, the more I wanted to tell their stories, too. After all, what is a Tour victory if you don't know who you've defeated? And the Tour is as much about the bit-part players as it is the General Classification contenders.

So as I ride my bike around the Chilterns, submitting meekly after just 50km, I think of how Roger Walkowiak could win a Tour 5,000km long and then be called lucky. Of how he could beat the World Champion, the Giro winner, and over 100 other men all seeking individual glory, and be saddled with one of the greatest insults in cycling. To win à la Walkowiak.

And so, I suggest that we reclaim the phrase à la Walkowiak: to win while nobody is looking.

And if it's the only success you have, then that's fine.

Praise for "We Rode All Day"

Cycling histories can prove a little dull, an overload of numbers, dates and places. We Rode All Day is literally a novel approach to the genre that adds an extra dimension, brings the personal suffering, the kindnesses, greed and glories to life.

Suspend your disbelief, hop into the saddle and ride the 1919 Tour with the men who were actually there.

Rolf Rae Hansen

We may have come a long way with our carbon fibre, garish lycra and slick gears, but cycling remains, at its heart, much the same as it did 100 years ago.

We Rode All Day brings all that to mind. Along with Tim Krabbé's The Racer it should become essential reading for anyone that rides a bike.

Robbie Broughton, RideVélo

www.ingramcontent.com/pod-product-compliance
Lightning Source LLC
Chambersburg PA
CBHW030000110526
44587CB00011BA/920